Palgrave Texts in Counselling and Psychotherapy

Series Editors
David Pocock, Psychoanalytic Psychotherapist and Systemic Family Therapist, Calne, Wiltshire, UK
Jeremy Woodcock, Holman's Cottage, Nailsworth, UK

This series introduces readers to the theory and practice of counselling and psychotherapy across a wide range of topical issues. Ideal for both trainees and practitioners, the books will appeal to anyone wishing to use counselling and psychotherapeutic skills and will be particularly relevant to workers in health, education, social work and related settings. The books in this series emphasise an integrative orientation weaving together a variety of models including, psychodynamic, attachment, trauma, narrative and systemic ideas. The books are written in an accessible and readable style with a focus on practice. Each text offers theoretical background and guidance for practice, with creative use of clinical examples.

Michelle Andrews Luke

A Guide to Relationship-Oriented Child Therapy

The Art of Listening for Connection

palgrave
macmillan

Michelle Andrews Luke
Faculty of Education
University of Melbourne
Parkville, VIC, Australia

ISSN 2662-9127 ISSN 2662-9135 (electronic)
Palgrave Texts in Counselling and Psychotherapy
ISBN 978-3-031-99657-3 ISBN 978-3-031-99658-0 (eBook)
https://doi.org/10.1007/978-3-031-99658-0

Cover credit: Roman Sigaev/Alamy Stock Photo

This Palgrave Macmillan imprint is published by the registered company Springer Nature Switzerland AG
The registered company address is: Gewerbestrasse 11, 6330 Cham, Switzerland

This book is lovingly dedicated to my children,
Madeleine, Isabelle, and Sebastian

Acknowledgements

My heartfelt thanks to my clients who have given me permission to share their encounters with me. I have changed names and identifying details to preserve confidentiality. I thank you all for the gift of your stories and shared experiences. Stories are the bridge that connects us all.

A special thanks to my dear mentor, Associate Professor Erica Frydenberg. You have been there every step of the way. Your enthusiastic support buoys me. It lifts me up.

Many thanks to my colleagues in the field: Dr Mary Ainley, Dr Louisa Hoey, Catriona O'Neill, Dr Annette Rome, Dr Steven Middleton, Sue Eden, Louise Sayar, Peter Robertson, David Bennett, Delanie Lewis, Brooke White, Bianca Moran, Sophie Healy, Dr Todd Zadow, Jo Cardullo, Allison Stekelenburg, Associate Professor Vicki McKenzie, Dr Chelsea Hyde, Dr Cheree Murrihy, Dr Georgia Dawson, Dr Ben Deery, Professor Kate Reynolds, Dr Jennifer Sze, Kelly Cooch, Sally Kenney, and Sarah Ballantyne-Brodie. I am grateful for your encouragement and friendship.

I am extremely lucky to have Murrundindi as a guide. Your wisdom runs through the pages of this book.

I also thank my students at the University of Melbourne. You helped me to find the courage to put my ideas on paper and to write my first book.

I would like to thank the team at Palgrave Macmillan, including Liam Inscoe-Jones, the commissioning editor, for recognising the value of this book. Thanks also to David Pocock, series editor, for your enthusiasm and for helping to bring my vision to life.

Thank you to my family for their love. My father, Mal, is a wise advisor. My mother, Karen, epitomises care and compassion, and my step-father, David, demonstrates kindness and generosity. My brother, Brett; my sister-in-law, Ash; my nephew, Roy; and my niece, Marlee, show me what it means to dance together through life with a smile. I thank all of you.

And, of course, I want to thank my three children, Madeleine, Isabelle, and Sebastian. You are the loves of my life. I admire you all for your warm heartedness and compassion. You teach me so much.

Most of all, I am grateful to my husband, Dr Michael Andrews Luke, my first reader of the entire manuscript. For more than thirty years, you have made me feel truly seen, heard, and understood. I feel incredibly lucky to be your life partner. Your presence and companionship mean everything to me.

Introduction

> Love is born into every human being; it calls back the halves of our original nature together; it tries to make one out of two and heal the wound of human nature.
> Plato

This book is about how child therapists can work with children, their families, and their teachers. Throughout the pages of this book, I share what I have learned in more than twenty years of helping children cope with stress, anxiety, and trauma. One of my main ideas is that positive relationships are essential for children's mental health and wellbeing. Abraham Maslow, in his theory of human needs, describes our need for love, affection, and belonging as fundamental (Maslow 1998; originally published in 1962). I believe that our deepest need is to be seen, heard, and accepted by others, and that my role as a child therapist is to listen to my clients and to help them to have strong and supportive relationships so that they may heal and thrive.

The idea that relationships are necessary for health and happiness is not a new one. Humans are social creatures, and we rely on connecting with others to survive and flourish. Australia's Aboriginal and Torres Strait Islander people have used yarning circles for thousands of years to help people find connection and hope. People sit together to talk and share stories. They listen deeply and learn from each other.

I offer my guidance in this book because I am concerned about the field of child therapy. Unfortunately, many graduate programs focus on one-on-one talk therapy. I believe that this approach is too narrow and neglects the vital importance of working together with the people who surround children. Talking in individual therapy can be very healing for children, but true healing extends beyond the therapy session; it occurs within the broader interconnectedness of each child's world.

I am also concerned that our children are in crisis. My clients tell me that they feel stressed and anxious about the future. They are worried about climate change, global conflict, and their mental health. They were isolated for weeks and months during the COVID-19 pandemic, and the effects are ongoing. One thing they share again and again, both directly and indirectly, is: "I feel lonely."

I argue in these pages that we need a new approach to child therapy that prioritises connections with others. I am not suggesting that we do away with individual therapy. As well as providing individual therapy to help our clients to feel accepted and less lonely, we can help the people who populate our clients' lives to relate well to our clients. Good relationships matter.

When I was about nine, my Year 4 teacher, Mrs Malone, gave my class a family tree project to complete. I drew a family tree with branches and leaves. I used Textas to draw the outline, a brown pencil to colour in the trunk, and a dark green pencil to colour in the leaves. When it came time to fill in the details and to add names, I asked my mother about my family history. I remember my mother telling me that my maternal grandmother was not her biological mother and that her biological mother abandoned her and her two younger siblings when she was five years old. I recall my mother telling me that her father had trouble keeping his head above water and that she was placed in foster care in a poor area of Melbourne. I can picture my mother saying that she reunited with her father and siblings at the age of nine. I can see a distant and faraway expression on her face as she speaks.

Painful things happened to my mother, and they left their mark. My mother struggles to talk about those times. I know that she felt neglected and invisible. Yet she carried on and has good relationships with her siblings, my stepfather, her stepchildren, my brother and me, our partners, and her grandchildren. For many years she worked as a cook, and I have images from my childhood of her bringing home muffins and pastries for me and my brother. I see her dancing and singing, *Always Look on the*

Bright Side of Life. I hear her saying that becoming a mother was the best day of her life. Like all of us, my mother has her flaws, but I feel deep admiration towards her for facing each day with a smile and for showering my brother and me with tenderness and motherly care, despite not being mothered herself. For a great many years, I have tried to work out my mother. How exactly did having a hard childhood affect her worldview? How did she become so strong and resilient?

One thing my mother taught me was that happiness is about connecting with others and caring for children. She says: "Kids just need to be loved and made to feel safe. If they are loved and feel safe, they can do anything." When I was at university, I decided to become a child therapist and work with children. I could spread the warmth she shared with me. I could help children to feel safe, seen, valued, and heard. Throughout my career, I have tried to find the best ways to relate to children and to listen well.

My discoveries over the years have been fairly straightforward. Treat children the way you would like to be treated. Show them respect and kindness. Be mindful of their feelings. Recognise that they deserve to be listened to.

I like acronyms, and I use the acronym NOVA to guide my work. I came up with the idea while overseeing a graduate student's research project at the University of Melbourne. We were looking at a lot of studies about how to listen effectively to children and identified four key elements. N stands for *nonverbal engagement* (e.g., be warm and lean forward); O for *openness and empathy* (e.g., be willing to enter the child's world); V for *verbal strategies* (e.g., ask the child good questions); and A for *attentiveness* (e.g., focus on the child and their feelings). All four of these critical components will be described at different points throughout this book.

I also like metaphors. A nova is a bright star. It brings clarity. Effective listening can shed light on a child's deepest thoughts and feelings and can help a child to feel seen. True listening also allows children to express their fullest selves and to heal. Thich Nhat Hanh, the Vietnamese Zen Buddhist monk, said: "Compassionate listening brings about healing. A good therapist always practices deep, compassionate listening" (Nhat Hanh 1999; p. 86). When children are listened to carefully and sensitively, it helps them to open up and grow. My goal when working with children, their parents, and teachers is to help cultivate nurturing relationships through good listening. It is the listening that leads to wellbeing. Listening to children is good for children.

When I was a beginning psychologist in the early 2000s, one of my mentors, Erica Frydenberg, recommended *The Gift of Therapy: Reflections on Being a Therapist* by eminent existential psychiatrist Irvin Yalom (Yalom 2002). This book consists of eighty-five tips for new therapists working with adults. I found the real case studies and personal reflections incredibly engaging and valuable, particularly in my work with adolescents on the cusp of adulthood. I was extremely fortunate to meet Yalom at the *Evolution of Psychotherapy Conference* in December 2005 and to thank him for sharing his advice and insights. From time to time, I reread *The Gift of Therapy*.

The author with Irvin Yalom December 2005

In these pages, I have put together my own fifty suggestions for beginning child therapists. My recommendations about how to listen well to children stem from my years of experience working with children, their families, and teachers, and my knowledge of what works. I am a trained educational and developmental psychologist, and I draw on the findings and theories of Carl R. Rogers, John Bowlby, Viktor Frankl, Uri Bronfenbrenner, Richard Ryan, Edward Deci, Daniel J. Siegel, Barbara Fredrickson, and other notable figures in the field of psychology. I incorporate concepts central to humanistic and positive psychology, including the notion that positive feelings, such as joy, interest, and love, promote growth and wellbeing. Throughout, I have attempted to write with the candour, authenticity, and relatability that characterises Yalom's work. I have also long admired the simple and direct writing style of American child and adolescent therapist Violet Oaklander and have tried to incorporate these elements into my writing.

I started planning this book in July 2024. I remember the day well. I was at my home in the Dandenong Ranges, a set of mountain ranges east of Melbourne. It was a chilly day, and our fire was burning. As I began to set down my thoughts, I looked out over a group of stringybark eucalyptus trees towards Mount Riddell and took a deep breath. I wrote on average for one to two days a week over a 10-month period in between my family life, my clinical work, and my teaching. I teach *Counselling Skills* and *Working with Groups* graduate courses within the Master of Psychology (Educational and Developmental) program at the University of Melbourne. Every time I wrote, I imagined that I was talking with my graduate students. They are compassionate, intelligent, diligent, and curious. Most of them are both excited and apprehensive as they start their professional journeys. They are eager to learn. This book grew out of the questions I am often asked by my students.

My suggestions are divided into four parts. *Part I: The Therapist* (Chapter 1) describes the inner work that child therapists must engage in to truly connect with children. *Part II: The Child* (Chapters 2–7) focuses on the child-therapist relationship and explores how to establish and maintain a strong connection with children in the therapy room. *Part III: The Family* (Chapters 8 and 9) discusses how to include parents and families in the therapeutic process and how to help them to relate better as a family. In *Part IV: The World* (Chapter 10), I describe how to connect each child's challenges and growth to the wider world and how to collaborate with teachers. When I say the word "child," I am referring to anyone under the age of 18. Each suggestion begins with one or two of my favourite quotes. Where possible, I have cited the source of each quote. Each suggestion title starts with a verb or action word because the content is about what child therapists can do.

It is my sincere hope that readers will find these tips useful. Each reader will have their own unique circumstances, background, and clients. I invite readers to pick and choose the suggestions that will be most appropriate for them given their particular circumstances. In my experience, therapists are generally busy people. The sections are deliberately short, and they are designed to be dipped into. I have grouped the tips according to the themes described above, but they do not need to be read in order. The book can be read from beginning to end or more casually. I encourage readers to choose sections based on personal interests and points of need. Whatever works best.

I am optimistic that there is a new generation of child therapists who understand the value of relationships and who want to learn more about relationship-oriented therapy. This book is for these therapists.

Contents

PART I

The Therapist

CHAPTER 1

The Inner Work of the Therapist

1 Make Time to Pause and Reflect

> Knowing yourself is the beginning of all wisdom.
> Aristotle

I begin my first class with my students by asking them the following questions: Why do you want to become a child therapist? Why children? Which life events or circumstances influenced your decision to become a therapist? What are you looking forward to most? What are your fears about becoming a therapist? What are your main strengths? Which strengths will support you in your goal of becoming an effective therapist? What is most important to you? What are your key values? Which values will serve you well as a therapist? Which values might get in the way? Of course, my aim in asking these questions is to help my students to develop a greater sense of self-awareness.

To be self-aware means to know yourself. To be self-reflective means to actively monitor yourself so that you can become more self-aware. The way I see things, regular opportunities to pause and reflect and to nurture the skills of self-awareness and self-reflection are the most important aspect of any therapy training program. These skills are essential. They allow us therapists to identify our own blind spots and any personal issues

M. Andrews Luke, *A Guide to Relationship-Oriented Child Therapy*, Palgrave Texts in Counselling and Psychotherapy,
https://doi.org/10.1007/978-3-031-99658-0_1

that might hinder our ability to truly understand and help our clients. They also enable us to see ourselves more clearly and to successfully use our own feelings during therapy sessions to navigate any therapy situation. Perhaps most importantly, these skills help us to bring our whole authentic selves into the therapy room and to have a genuine relationship with our clients. In their book, *Master Therapists*, psychologists and counselling expertise researchers Thomas Skovholt and Len Jennings write that therapists who are deemed to be "the best of the best" by their colleagues:

> ...appear to be quite reflective and self-aware and use these attributes to continue to learn and grow personally and professionally. These master therapists seem to possess emotional maturity and strength of character that comes from years of active learning and living. Finally, the master therapists appear to be able to relate superbly to others, which, one can assume, often leads to a strong working alliance and positive therapeutic outcomes. (Skovholt and Jennings 2016) (p. 49)

How can you become a more introspective therapist? Try asking yourself why you are a child therapist. Regularly reflect on all that you do. Seek out new learning experiences. Read widely. Attend seminars, workshops, and conferences. Present at conferences. Become a member of professional organisations and go along to their events. These are the places where important topics are explored by the "best of the best." There is much collective wisdom. Be sure to build relationships at these events with like-minded colleagues. Being a therapist can be isolating. Coming together with peers confronting similar issues can help us to more closely examine our own experiences, to bring things into focus, to grow and learn, and to feel a sense of belonging. For example, I am an active member of the Australian Psychological Society (APS), the APS College of Educational and Developmental Psychologists, and the APS College of Counselling Psychologists. Being an engaged member of professional organisations provides a powerful route to self-inquiry about one's own beliefs and practices.

See if you can set aside time to write about your experiences. I often feel the need to spend time alone with my thoughts and to consider the many aspects of my work and the direction of my professional life. Make a list of your professional hopes for the future. Ask yourself: What is really important to me? How will I get there? Does my vision reflect my true values?

When therapists are starting out, they often get caught up in getting things done and leave precious little room for focused contemplation. Self-reflection is about making the time to look inward. It is a conscious decision to dwell within ourselves. To make self-reflection a part of our lives requires commitment and dedication. Some may protest that they don't have enough time. But I would suggest that being self-reflective and self-aware amounts to behaving professionally. We can only connect deeply with the children we are working with if we are deeply connected to our own selves. It is a great gift to look deeply into ourselves and to examine who we really are.

2 Enter Your Own Therapy

> Forget your perfect offering
> There is a crack, a crack in everything
> That's how the light gets in.
> Leonard Cohen, *Anthem*
> (Cohen 1992)

One of the best ways to get in touch with our feelings and ourselves is to participate in our own therapy. Taking the time to sit down and contemplate our lives and who we are helps us to see ourselves as we actually are. It is a commonly held view that therapists have it all together. The children and the families we work with can sometimes put us on a pedestal. While it is true that we have expertise in mental health and wellbeing, we are full human beings. We have the same struggles and foibles as everyone else. We child therapists must recognise and accept our whole selves, including our fears and our flaws, to be able to have genuine empathy for our clients. Personal therapy enables us to cultivate a compassionate and generous attitude towards ourselves and others.

I have participated in my own therapy at many different times in my life. During my training, I had a brief period of therapy at my university counselling centre. When my children were very young, I had a near-death experience, and I experienced substantial feelings of death anxiety. I decided to have a one-year course of therapy. I felt terrified at the prospect of dying while my children were so young, and I knew that I had to have therapy if I was to continue to work with children myself. I've had stretches of online therapy and therapy by texting, and I've been a member of support groups with other child therapists. I've participated in therapist-led women's groups, parent groups, mindfulness groups, and art therapy groups.

These therapy experiences have been profoundly valuable. They have enabled me to see and know myself better, including my dark side, and to feel more at home in my skin. They have also helped me to become better at staying with my clients and their pain and to act with greater clarity. Perhaps most importantly, they have allowed me to know for myself how therapy works from the perspective of the client. Only by engaging in one's own therapy can one truly understand what it's like to be a client and how much effort it requires. It can take a whole lot of courage just to walk into the therapy room.

A great many of my students say that they decided to become child therapists because they had a positive experience of therapy as a child. They explain that it gave them strength, and that they want to provide the same safe and supportive space for their clients. I encourage them to re-enter therapy during their training and at other stages of their career. Gerald Corey, the American psychologist and author of many counselling textbooks, goes as far as to suggest that training programs should require students to engage in their own therapy. In his words, "A rationale for this requirement rests on the assumption that we cannot take our clients further in their journey than we have gone ourselves" (Corey 2020; p. 61). If you do decide to enter therapy, allow yourself to be truly open about your feelings. Be willing to face your own darkness and despair. By relating to our own suffering, we can relate more easily to the suffering of our clients.

3 Develop Your Own Integrative Perspective

Be yourself; everyone else is already taken.
Oscar Wilde

When I was starting out as a practicing therapist, the most valuable conference I attended was the *Evolution of Psychotherapy Conference* in Anaheim, California, in December 2005. It was a remarkable meeting. More than 8,000 people attended. I remember listening to the founder of rational emotive behaviour therapy (REBT), Albert Ellis, give a feisty presentation on how to help clients change self-defeating thoughts, feelings, and behaviours: “It’s never the things that happen to you that upset you; it’s your view of them…no matter how bad life is, and it sometimes is very bad…you accept it the way it is and you make the most of what you can.” The originator of cognitive therapy, Aaron Beck, shared his ideas and recollections about the development of cognitive therapy. The creator of structural family therapy, Salvador Minuchin, gave a lively demonstration of a family therapy session. One of the co-founders of cognitive-behavioural therapy (CBT), Donald Meichenbaum, discussed working with suicidal clients. Irvin Yalom spoke of the therapist-client relationship from an existential therapy perspective: “The therapist with increased existential sensibility will see there’s no real clear boundary between them and the afflicted…everyone, and that includes therapists, is destined to experience not only the exhilaration of life but it’s inevitable despair.” The founder of multimodal therapy, Arnold Lazarus, described the basics of multimodal therapy and the common mistakes that most therapists make. One of the co-creators of narrative therapy, Michael White, discussed “maps of narrative practice” or ways that people can explore the territories of their lives. The father of the newly created field of positive psychology, Martin Seligman, gave presentations on happiness and talked about “finding out what your highest strengths and talents are…and then recrafting your relationships with other people…to use those things more.”

I was fascinated by the stories and anecdotes they shared. Up until that point, I had mostly learned about their approaches via secondary sources, such as textbooks. Hearing these master therapists speak humanised their theories. As I listened to them talk, it became obvious that their theoretical frameworks were all based on their specific contexts and life experiences. For example, Albert Ellis shared his story of facing his fear of rejection by women by approaching 100 women in the Bronx Botanical Gardens, and he noted that the experience of forcing himself to do the thing he feared most had contributed to the development of his principles and practices of REBT: “I talked to all of them…I got completely over my fear of talking to women in strange places.” It was exceedingly evident to me that their models of therapy did not emerge in a vacuum.

I also came away from the conference struck by the similarities between the approaches. Despite their different terminology, the presenters all referred to listening respectfully to their clients. They all touched on the therapeutic relationship between the therapist and client. Another common element highlighted by all was the importance of practicing new behaviours. And all of the presenters clearly cared deeply about helping their clients. I came to the realisation then and there that there were common aspects of all of the approaches that I found appealing, and that it would be wise to draw from different therapy orientations in my future clinical practice.

Historically, therapists were trained in a single school of therapy. However, more and more therapists are working from an integrative perspective. In the words of psychologists John Norcross and Erin Alexander, there has been "a rapid increase in integrative therapies of late" (Norcross and Alexander 2019; p. 5). Norcross and Alexander offer a number of reasons for this increase, including the proliferation of more than 500 therapies, the recognition that no one approach is suitable for all clients and for all situations, and the failure of research to conclusively demonstrate that any single school is superior or more effective than the others. They also point to research which has found that one of the most significant factors influencing the success of therapy is the therapy relationship.

As you start your clinical practice, I encourage you to develop an integrative perspective. Study all of the main theories and read the original works. Go to the source. Original books and papers provide an unfiltered description of the theories. What are their strengths and limitations? Watch videos of the founders of the various therapeutic approaches in practice. I have found it helpful to watch the videos on Psychotherapy.net. There are also many videos freely available on YouTube. Which theoretical principles or methods resonate with you most? Why? What do they have in common? How are they connected? Which therapeutic techniques do you believe would work best given the needs of the children you are working with? Over time, you will develop and refine your own personal therapeutic orientation.

4 Get a Mentor

> Teach them the quiet words of kindness, to live beyond themselves. Urge them toward excellence, drive them toward gentleness, pull them deep into yourself, pull them upward toward manhood, but softly like an angel arranging clouds. Let your spirit move through them softly.
> Pat Conroy, *The Prince of Tides* (p. 74)
> (Conroy 1991)

The word "mentor" has its origins in Homer's ancient Greek poem, *The Odyssey* (Homer 1966; originally composed eighth or seventh century BCE). When Odysseus, King of Ithaca, sets out for the Trojan War, he leaves his friend Mentor in charge of his household and the education of his son, Telemachus. However, Mentor provides little genuine guidance or wisdom to Telemachus in Odysseus's long absence. At one point, the goddess Athene intervenes and appears in the form of Mentor to counsel Telemachus directly:

> For yourself, here is my advice. It is sound, and I hope you will take it. Choose your best ship, man her with twenty oars, and set out to discover why your father has been gone for so long...You, my friend – and what a tall and splendid fellow you have grown! – must be as brave as Orestes. (pp. 32–33)

Telemachus responds by saying:

> ...you have spoken to me out of the kindness of your heart like a father talking to his son; and I shall never forget your words. (p. 33)

It is Athene, not Mentor, who acts as a wise mentor for Telemachus. Athene is Telemachus's champion and protector.

Like most ancient stories, *The Odyssey* is wise and provides us with a roadmap for living. It reminds us that it is worth seeking a mentor to help find our way. We don't always know where we are going. The best mentors remind us of our options and keep us on the path.

Many mentors have assisted me on my professional journey. In mid-December 1999, when I was a young psychology student at the University of Melbourne, I was given the names of three faculty members to contact as potential Honours supervisors. I reached out to them via email to introduce myself and to set up meetings. I met first with Mary Ainley. I've never forgotten standing outside Mary's office in the Redmond Barry Building as I waited for our meeting to start. I heard her speaking quietly to another student, who seemed upset. Mary, a distinguished developmental and educational psychology researcher and teacher known for her work on curiosity and interest, was so caring and engaged. I was struck by her kindness and generosity. I wanted to have Mary as my Honours supervisor! I was so pleased when Mary agreed to supervise me for both my Honours and Doctor of Educational Psychology courses. Mary was my first model of what it means to be a wise and compassionate professional in our field.

My second model was Erica Frydenberg. As well as Mary, I worked under the guidance of Erica during my doctoral studies. Erica, a revered educational, clinical, and organisational psychologist and researcher, was one of the founders of the study of child and adolescent coping. Countless people have commented on Erica's warm and welcoming way of being, her intellectual rigour, and her energy. Erica is a fine human being who embodies what it means to have a positive outlook and to live a life of resilience and wellbeing. Erica became a major influence on me, and her ideas about how to help children to cope well set me on my life's path. Erica has taught me many important things, including the value of enjoying the journey. I continue to see Erica every month or so, and her very presence is nourishing. We have long discussions about my work, and she radiates an optimism that invigorates me.

Mentoring is a relationship. The best mentors do not give you the answers. They create a nurturing space where your own ideas can emerge. They listen deeply. They communicate a deep belief in you and your abilities, and they help you to see the ways in which you can follow your passions and dreams. I encourage you to seek out multiple mentors during your career as a child therapist rather than limiting yourself to just one. As well as Mary and Erica, I have sought out different mentors at different stages in my professional life. In their own ways, they have all helped me to have the courage to be true to myself and to do what is really important to me, especially when the path seemed unclear.

5 Take Care of Yourself

If your compassion does not include yourself, it is incomplete.
Jack Kornfield, *Buddha's Little Instruction Book* (p. 28)
(Kornfield 1994)

Being a child therapist can be very demanding. It is a high-pressure job. Difficulties of all shapes and sizes pop up all the time. Our clients carry big burdens. Some are suicidal. We bear witness to their pain. Working with parents adds an extra layer of complexity. Another challenge is keeping up with our notes. We can also have our notes subpoenaed. Early on in my career, when I was working in some of the wealthiest areas of Sydney, Australia, I had client notes subpoenaed quite a few times due to custody disputes. I remember feeling worried that the notes would be taken out of context. I found the whole process of handing over the notes incredibly time-consuming and draining. Overall, though, I find that the most emotionally challenging part of my job is supporting abused and traumatised children. On occasion, I have cried at the end of the day.

Therapist stress is also related to years of practice and one's own history of trauma. Clinical psychologists and researchers Laurie Anne Pearlman and Paula Mac Ian looked at the impact of vicarious traumatisation on trauma therapists and found that newer therapists and those with a personal trauma history were most vulnerable (Pearlman and Mac Ian 1995). In her book, *Letters to a Young Therapist*, American psychologist and author Mary Pipher reminds us that many therapists are what Carl G. Jung referred to as "wounded healers" (Pipher 2016; originally published in 2003). We might have been drawn to becoming a therapist because of our own wounds. We might use our own pain and understanding to help others. But if we do not prioritise caring for ourselves, we will burn out, and we won't be able to care for others. Self-care is essential!

We must come up with our own strategies for coping with stress and maintaining our energy. In their book, *The Resilient Practitioner*, psychologists Thomas Skovholt and Michelle Trotter-Mathison write about "how to have an open heart without becoming trapped in the quicksand of human despair" (Skovholt and Trotter-Mathison 2025; p. 5). They suggest having what they call "Boundaried Generosity" (p. 5). This is about balancing self-care with other-care or balancing self-preservation with altruism.

I encourage you to put together a list of things you can do to look after yourself and to be clear about your boundaries. What are your boundaries? What is a reasonable number of sessions for you to have each day? What is a reasonable number of hours for you to work each week? What types of cases are you willing to take on? Your answers to these questions will change over your career depending on what is happening in your life. I recommend limiting your sessions to no more than six per day and saying no to unreasonable requests. Practice saying no. I confess to being a work in progress on this front. I find that I don't say no enough, but when I do, it's so worth the effort.

Pay particular attention to slowing things down outside of work. Set aside time to just be. I like having a bath once a week and getting a massage when I can. Taking it slow helps to take the edge off. It also helps to laugh. My husband Michael makes me laugh. As I write this, I am aware of how blessed I've been to have had Michael by my side since I was 16, so funny, intelligent, and loving. I feel so fortunate to have had him in my corner during good times and bad.

Think carefully about what you will do in hard times. Plan ahead if you can. Long ago, my mentor Erica Frydenberg suggested that I keep a folder of client thank you messages. When I have a particularly difficult day at work, I take them out and they remind me of the positive moments. I work in a small team of therapists, and I can call on them any time. They give me comfort and understanding. I also have an informal arrangement with a couple of colleagues and close friends from my training days, Louisa Hoey and Catriona O'Neill. We call each other if we've had a tough day. We have what we call "walk and talks": we walk outdoors while we talk. The combination of sharing my struggles with my peers, moving, and being in nature helps me to reset and replenish.

In mid-2018, I went to a workshop by self-compassion researcher Kristin Neff. Self-compassion is a type of self-care, but it is more of an attitude of kindness towards oneself rather than specific actions or behaviours. Kristen spoke of the importance of "treating yourself with the same kindness and care and tenderness when you're suffering that you would show to a good friend." Kristin also shared a mantra that she uses to remind herself to be self-compassionate when things go wrong:

> This is a moment of suffering.
> Suffering is part of life.
> May I be kind to myself in this moment.
> May I give myself the compassion I need.
> (Neff 2011) (p. 119)

Whenever things get intense, I repeat Kristin's mantra to myself. I find it soothing.

A final word on self-care: don't forget to savour the joys. Our work as child therapists can feel overwhelming and sometimes quite isolating, but working with children is a gift. Every day, I feel blessed to be entrusted with the private stories of my clients and to make so many close connections. There is nothing more satisfying than helping others through their struggles. My clients have taught me so much. I've learned an enormous amount about what it means to be human and how to be present. Being open to the lessons of my clients has nurtured my own growth. What a delight it is to be a child therapist. Remind yourself of the privileges whenever you can.

PART II

The Child

CHAPTER 2

Establishing the Therapeutic Relationship

1 Introduce What Happens in Therapy

> As we entered the room I said, 'We'll spend an hour together here in the playroom. You can see the toys and materials we have. You decide what you would like to do.'
> Virgina M. Axline, *Dibs in Search of Self* (p. 22)
> (Axline 1990; originally published in 1964)

Most of the children I see are brought to therapy by their parents. Teenagers often instigate therapy themselves. Some come to therapy due to a specific event, such as divorce, death of a loved one, or a disaster. Many parents seek help for their child because their situation has become very challenging at home or at school. Frequently, parents will say that their child's behaviour has become intolerable. Their child might be having meltdowns, hitting other children, refusing to go to school, or fearful of trying new things. The mother of a 9-year-old boy who was struggling to start unfamiliar tasks told me that her son was "stubborn when he was in that zone."

M. Andrews Luke, *A Guide to Relationship-Oriented Child Therapy*, Palgrave Texts in Counselling and Psychotherapy,
https://doi.org/10.1007/978-3-031-99658-0_2

Despite this focus on behaviour, many of my clients' difficulties are the result of problems in the realm of relationships. Some behave aggressively because of deep feelings of rejection. Others talk as little as possible because they feel different from everyone else and are afraid to open up. Often, they have received the message that difficult feelings—like sadness and anger—are unacceptable, which makes it harder for them to fully experience their feelings and to express their feelings to others directly, causing a greater sense of isolation.

Given this, one of my goals is to help each child to connect with themselves and their feelings through their relationship with me so that they can establish stronger connections with others. More than twenty years ago, Irvin Yalom noted that "the intimate and caring therapeutic relationship that does not result in the anticipated catastrophe becomes a corrective emotional experience" (Yalom 2002, p. 11). Therapy is an art, and each therapist will create a supportive relationship with each client in their own way. I begin the therapy process by introducing myself to my clients and describing what happens in therapy. For example:

> We might do things together like drawing, painting, using clay, reading books, and talking. What's important for you to know is that this is your time. Sometimes I might invite you to do a drawing, or we might read a book together or we might talk. You get to choose. Sometimes we will talk about feelings. My job is to listen to you. It is also important for us to work together and to build a good relationship with each other, and I will often ask you how *we* are going. Most children I see say that it helps. You are welcome to have a look around at the things in my office and choose what you want to do.

Through these words of introduction, my clients discover that I respect them and that I take them seriously, which is at the heart of any therapeutic relationship with children. Children do not have as much power as adults, and their opinions are often dismissed. Anyone who works with children needs to value children and their right to be heard. What matters in child therapy is that each child feels like they matter.

2 Tune in to Each Child

In times of stress, the best thing we can do for each other is to listen with our ears and our hearts and to be assured that our questions are just as important as our answers.
Fred Rogers

One of the first steps in therapy is to establish rapport. This is only possible when we understand child development and how children of different ages think, communicate, and relate to others. Developmental psychology tells us that by three years of age, most children can have a simple conversation but are easily distracted; that by five years of age, most children can understand "why" questions and the concept of time; that by eight years of age, most children can use language in an abstract way; and that by 11 years of age, most children can have deep conversations. Almost all children communicate their feelings, thoughts, and experiences through play, especially when they do not have the words.

Sometimes my students ask me what they should say when first meeting with a particular child. I explain that I never know exactly how I will express myself beforehand, and that children are the best teachers. I am tuned in to their tone of voice, facial expressions, and movements. How do they respond to me? Do they ask questions? What is their behaviour telling me about what I can realistically expect from them? I use these cues to determine how to connect with my clients and what techniques to use.

For example, a six-year-old girl, Emma, was brought in to see me because her mother had died unexpectedly. Emma walked into my office and told me clearly that, "My Mum died. I am my Mum's daughter. My Mum's name is Sarah." Emma looked up at me tentatively: how would I respond? I met her eyes, and I gave her a tub of clay and asked, "Would you like to make a clay model of your Mum?" She nodded and brightened up as she worked.

"Are there certain things that are important to include to make it really look like your Mum?" I asked.

"Long hair," she announced.

"Can you share a special memory about your Mum?" I asked.

"Me and my Mum once went to Gumbuya World!" she exclaimed.

This child had been feeling weighed down by grief. Making a clay model of her Mum and my questions gave her permission to enjoy the positive memories of her Mum alongside her feelings of sadness.

"How does it make you feel to make this?" I asked.

"Very sad and happy."

All child therapists will develop their own methods of joining with children that are just right for each child. This may include playing card games, drawing, or using music. In my view, what happens in those first minutes is critical. Anyone who knows children knows that they are tuned into adults' behaviour and are quick to form impressions. Is this someone I can begin to trust?

3 Radiate Warmth

> First is a warmth and responsiveness on the part of the counselor, which makes rapport possible, and which gradually develops into a deeper emotional relationship.
> Carl R. Rogers, *Counseling and Psychotherapy* (p. 87)
> (Rogers 1942)

In the 1940s, Carl R. Rogers described the basic qualities that characterise the most supportive therapeutic relationships, including warmth and acceptance. Good therapists convey care and genuine interest. In my work with children, I make sure to express kindness by addressing each child by their name, by offering them a glass of water, and by using a gentle tone of voice. Children often rely on non-verbal cues to feel safe and supported, such as open body language, eye contact, and sincere smiles. Some child therapists communicate affection by offering a comforting physical gesture. I make it a priority to sit close to my clients and to lean in slightly. Many times I have ended a therapy session with a pat on the shoulder or a handshake. We humans have a deep need for direct, personal interactions with others in real time.

The researcher and psychologist Barbara Fredrickson suggests that these micro-moments of interpersonal connection help people to feel truly connected, and that expressions of warmth and openness by one person evoke feelings of warmth and openness in the other person (Fredrickson 2013). Building on findings from neuroscience, Fredrickson writes in her book *Love 2.0* that these moments of "positivity resonance" confer many benefits to both the recipient and the person who initiates these gestures, including more positive emotions, expanded awareness, and increased resilience.

When we therapists demonstrate warmth and openness, our clients feel more comfortable opening up themselves and are better able to explore the difficult areas of their lives and to connect with us, which helps them to feel calmer. An example: Mila, a 14-year-old client, had a history of family conflict. She felt overwhelmed, confused, and alone. In our initial session, as she quietly described her family situation and her feelings of despair, I leaned in, nodded my head, and reached both hands out towards her, literally opening my arms out wide to communicate my feelings of warmth and acceptance of her as a person.

In our second session, she felt safe enough to accept my bids for connection, and she opened up more.

"I think about cutting myself. The main thing that stops me is that people might notice. I feel so powerless and worthless," Mila said.

Later on, I asked her to pick an object that best described herself.

"A piece of broken glass," said Mila. She looked towards the glass of water on the table between us, and tears slipped down her cheeks.

"Is there something wrong with me?" she asked.

Filled with feelings of rejection and self-doubt, Mila had been reluctant to share her sense of shame until now, believing that she was beyond repair and unlovable. I did not hesitate to say that Mila's thoughts and feelings were normal given her circumstances, and that she mattered a great deal to many, including myself and her teachers. This was a powerful moment, leading to a deeper sense of connection between us and greater trust in future sessions. Therapist openness results in client openness.

The world has changed significantly over the past decade or so. Social psychologist Jonathan Haidt laments the loss of a play-based childhood and the shift to a phone-based childhood (Haidt 2024). Increasingly, children are more likely to connect to others online, often asynchronously, and not in person, and to experience loneliness. This makes it all the more important for those of us working with children to be in the same physical space as our clients, to mirror their facial expressions and movements, and to cultivate moments of heartfelt warmth and tenderness. By doing this, we can do much to alleviate feelings of isolation and to give our clients hope.

In one of our final sessions, I asked Mila what had been most helpful about therapy. Like most clients who are asked this question, Mila said that she "felt supported" by me. First and foremost, our clients value our supportive presence rather than our suggestions or observations. What lingers is the human element. Mila also said that we were "on the same wavelength." As she spoke, her words reminded me of a singing duet I had recently observed. In my mind's eye, I could see the two performers standing close together, their voices harmonising. Synchronised movements, highlighting the warmth, rapport, and connection between them, much like our close and caring client-therapist relationship.

4 Be Authentic

> This above all: to thine own self be true.
> William Shakespeare, *Hamlet* (Act 1, scene 3, line 78)
> (Shakespeare 2015; originally published in 1599)
> To be yourself in a world that is constantly trying to make you something else is the greatest accomplishment.
> Ralph Waldo Emerson

Adults often use exaggerated or high-pitched voices when speaking to children. Perhaps they do this to try to make what they are saying seem more engaging or to make themselves seem more friendly. When my children were young, I remember watching children's TV shows with them and wincing at certain TV hosts. Their voices were always perky and excitable, which I found strange and unnatural and often patronising. To my mind, using a false tone of voice with children is an example of inauthenticity and is counterproductive. Think of your own experiences watching people talk in commercials. Do their voices and personalities often seem exaggerated and contrived, and do they seem phony and dubious to you? In contrast, think of your experiences being with the people you trust the most. Chances are, they use their real voices, and you feel like you really know them, and you feel close to them.

Over the years, I have tried to develop my own voice and to express what I truly feel, think, and know with my clients. Communicating my true feelings in an authentic way can be a struggle at times, but I have found that saying what I really think in a genuine tone of voice is much more likely to create a trusting relationship between myself and my clients and to facilitate personal growth and development in my clients. Carl R. Rogers writes that when therapists are themselves and when there is alignment between their inner feelings and their outward behaviour—when they are being "congruent"—therapy is more likely to be successful (Rogers 1961). I personally prefer to use the term "authentic," which comes from the Greek word "authentikos" and means being real and true, because I think it better captures the broader quality of being our genuine, true, and whole selves with our clients. If we can be authentic with our clients, then our clients can be who they truly are, openly and transparently.

In our digital age, where digital platforms seem to encourage the sharing of idealised images of girls who are softly spoken and adorable, I am seeing more girls who seem inauthentic and false. I once encountered an 11-year-old girl, Chloe, who was referred to me because she had a nervous stomach. Her parents had recently separated, and she had learning difficulties. She seemed meek and sweet, and she always used an upbeat and sing-song voice. In our third session, she cried for the first time when she shared that she had been bullied online by her peers. She seemed shocked and angry as she described their hateful comments. I encouraged her to stay with her feelings by inviting her to talk about her feelings using *The Bears* (2022), which are a set of cards showing bears expressing feelings in different ways. I also reflected back to her that she seemed to be expressing her deepest feelings, and I was willing myself to be explicit about my feelings.

"While you've been describing what it was like to read their comments, and how they affected you, I somehow feel like I understand who you really are much, much better."

"I feel sad and hurt," she replied, in a forlorn and somber voice.

Humanistic psychologist Scott Barry Kaufman states in his book *Transcend* that the key ingredients of healthy authenticity are self-awareness, self-honesty, integrity, and authentic relationships (Kaufman 2020). Being authentic—being in touch with my true beliefs about Chloe's behaviour and making a point to express them for the benefit of our relationship—helped Chloe to shed her façade and be more open and honest with me and to connect with and give voice to parts of herself that had previously been suppressed. It was the beginning of her personal journey towards growth and much deeper relationships. In psychoanalyst Karen Horney's view, the real self, "that central inner force, common to all human beings and yet unique in each…is the deep source of growth" (Horney 1991; originally published in 1950, p. 17). Strive to use your true voice with your clients. Be real and be transparent. Authentic therapists result in authentic clients.

5 Listen Deeply

> I am listening to him not only because I want to know what is inside him or to give him advice. I am listening to him just because I want to relieve his suffering.
> Thich Nhat Hahn, *The Heart of the Buddha's Teaching (p. 88)*
> (Nhat Hanh 1999)

My main task when working with children is to listen. Many people think of listening as simply being quiet while the other person talks, but that is not correct. Listening is much more than just being silent and passive. The Old English word for listen, hlysnan [HLEES-nahn], encompasses both hearing and actively paying attention. Listening is not just about hearing sounds: listening means focusing attention on what is being said.

Thich Nhat Hanh wrote that the most profound gift we can give anyone is our attention and proposed the practice of "deep listening." For Nhat Hanh, deep listening is about being fully present and listening with compassion and respect. When teaching about deep listening, Nhat Hanh emphasised that the purpose of deep listening is to help the other person to suffer less, and he noted that caring for others and listening to them in a deep way is also caring for ourselves, since we are all interconnected. Deep listening opens our hearts and helps to nourish our own wellbeing.

What does deep listening look like in practice when engaging with children? There are many preliminary steps that I find useful. I make certain to close my eyes and to take a few breaths before each session. I leave a gap between sessions. I try to eliminate distractions, like phones and notifications. My office is in an apartment in a two-story red brick building with a terracotta roof, and I look out over an elm tree, a lilly pilly tree, and a wisteria covered walkway. It is mostly quiet and free of noise. When children begin to share their stories, I make efforts to let go of any preconceived ideas about them, and to listen to them with my whole body. I concentrate on their words, energy, and presence. What are they trying to say about who they are, and what concerns them?

I also pay close attention to my own feelings, and I try not to get caught up in opinions about what my clients are saying. For example, about 10 years ago I worked with a 16-year-old girl, Jackie, who spoke bitterly about the way she had previously been treated by several peers at school, particularly her former close friend, Olive. Though satisfied with her relationships with her current friends, Jackie found it difficult to let go of her anger towards Olive. In one session, she described her rage towards Olive for being recognised at school as a great athlete. Jackie complained that Olive lacked integrity, and rambled about the unjustness of it all. As she spoke, she also implied that I had provided minimal assistance to her, and I could sense her irritation towards me. I felt exasperated and worn out by her hostility and resentment, and I found myself drifting away from the present moment and falling prey to negative opinions about her. What was I to do in this situation? I surveyed what was going on inside of me, I took a deep breath, and I reminded myself that my most important task was to listen and to help Jackie to feel seen, heard, and understood. I also reminded myself of Nhat Hanh's central idea, which is that even an hour of deep listening can bring profound transformation and healing. This helped me to get back in touch with each moment with Jackie and to let go of my negative opinions of her.

It is important to acknowledge that being fully present is demanding, especially when we work with very troubled clients. I believe that practicing mindfulness contributes greatly to our capacity to be more in touch with each moment. In my opinion, the best child therapists are those who actively cultivate mindfulness to enhance their therapeutic presence. Jon Kabat Zin has authored many books about mindfulness and his teachings have contributed enormously to the popularity of mindfulness in Western societies. According to Kabat-Zinn, mindfulness—which means paying attention intentionally, in the here-and-now, and without judgement—can be developed by engaging in a formal meditation practice and by seeking to bring mindfulness into every area of our lives (Kabat-Zinn 1994). He notes that the ability to watch our thoughts without being drawn into them allows us to be more in touch with our own deepest nature and wisdom. I have found that one simple way to nurture mindfulness is to set aside 10 minutes at the beginning of each day to just breathe. I also set aside time each week to swim, and I try to bring my attention to my breath and to observe my body while swimming. It is not easy, and my mind drifts, but these practices help me in my attempts to be more fully present with my clients, to feel calm, to see previously unseen connections, and to be more creative. You might ask yourself: how can I bring mindfulness into my life and into my everyday work? There is no greater gift that we can give to the children we work with than to be present for them.

CHAPTER 3

Core Therapeutic Techniques

1 Ask Good Questions

> Most of the time, therapy is this simple. One person agrees to listen and ask good questions while another explores his/her situation.
> Mary Pipher, *The Shelter of Each Other* (p. 147)
> (Pipher 1996)

Young children have many fears. They have fears of the dark, of monsters under the bed, of being separated from their parents, and of doctors and injections. Older children and teenagers have fears of being alone, being teased, fears of embarrassment and failure, and fears about the future. When children share their fears, many parents admonish them and say, "Don't be silly." Children are dependent on their parents, and most children do not want to upset their parents, so they often hide their fears from their parents. Good therapy is about helping children to bring their fears out in the open by being non-judgemental, listening well, and asking good questions.

How can we go about asking good questions? I have found that an effective exercise is to invite children to make shapes or figures out of Play-Doh to represent the different feelings they might be feeling and to ask thoughtful questions as they work. In the initial session, I might say: "Can you make shapes or figures that show how you feel when you

M. Andrews Luke, *A Guide to Relationship-Oriented Child Therapy*, Palgrave Texts in Counselling and Psychotherapy,
https://doi.org/10.1007/978-3-031-99658-0_3

are happy, sad, angry, and worried?" I usually invite children to make a happy shape or figure first because it is easier. I find that most children are enthusiastic about using Play-Doh. I make a point of sculpting the Play-Doh alongside the children. We usually work on a wooden table inside my office. Occasionally, we go outside and sit on the verandah.

Recall Chloe, the girl who had been referred to me because she had a nervous stomach. In one session, I said, "I know that your Dad isn't living with you anymore. Would you like to use the Play-Doh to let me know how you feel?" Chloe became absorbed in making different shapes and figures. She made a pink heart to represent happiness, a blue dog to represent sadness, a frowning red figure of herself to represent anger, and a falling purple wall to represent fear.

"Happiness is a heart," she said.

I asked, "Would you like to share more? What makes you feel happy?"

"Painting and being with my cousin," she called out.

"Tell me about your dog," I said.

"My Mum has to sell my dog when we move house," she said.

"Tell me about the red figure. What makes you feel angry?"

"When another girl tells me to stop acting dumb when I don't know the answer to a question, and I don't know the answer," she said quietly.

"Mmm," I said. "Tell me about the wall. What makes you feel worried?" I asked.

"Moving house at the end of the year," she whispered.

As well as asking children to tell me more and to tell me what makes them feel a particular way, I often ask them to imagine what they want their life to look like and to then make it: "I wonder what you wish for?" My aim is to help children to feel more hopeful. When I asked Chloe this question, she made a smiling orange Play-Doh figure of herself dancing. Using Play-Doh or other hands-on materials as a starting point helps children to begin to express themselves in a concrete, physical way. The best questions then help children to get more in touch with themselves, their feelings, and their own inner wisdom. Importantly, they also send the message that we are genuinely interested in them, that we want to learn more, and that we take them seriously.

The literature of listening supports the notion that good questions—along with eye contact and nodding—are closely linked to good listening (Bodie, Clyr et al. 2012). Why, exactly, are engaging questions considered so impactful? In a 2021 study, Netta Weinstein and her colleagues (Weinstein, Itzchakov and Legate 2021) linked high quality listening, such as asking open-ended and clarifying questions, to Richard Ryan and Edward

Deci's self-determination theory (Ryan and Deci 2017), which itself asks the question: what do people really need to flourish? At its core, self-determination theory suggests that flourishing occurs when we have three key psychological needs met: autonomy, competence, and relatedness. Drawing on Weinstein's research, I believe that the best questions help children to feel autonomous (as opposed to feeling controlled), competent (or effective), and a sense of relatedness (or connectedness). Good questions help us to create a human connection with our clients.

Like many therapists, I often ask the following question towards the end of each session: "Is there anything else you would like to share with me today?" I find it particularly useful. To illustrate: a 14-year-old girl named Hailey was brought to my office one day, clearly in shock. She had experienced a terrifying situation. She had been harassed by a much older man over multiple days as she walked home from school. She cried quietly and said that she no longer felt safe. When I asked her if there was anything else she would like to share, she said, "You know what, I am angry, and I want him caught and punished." I could feel her relief at sharing her feelings of rage. This question brought us closer together and reminded me why good questions matter.

2 Step into Each Child's Shoes

> You never really understand a person until you consider things from his point of view…until you climb into his skin and walk around in it.
> Harper Lee, *To Kill a Mockingbird* (p. 35)
> (Lee 1974; originally published in 1960)

Some adults find it difficult to truly grasp and connect with the inner lives of children. This might be because children's thoughts, feelings, and perspectives can seem small and inconsequential. It might also be because adults can sometimes have a hard time remembering their own childhoods. One of our most important tasks as child therapists is to seek to understand each child's experiences and to enter their worlds. Walking alongside our clients and offering our clients "accurate empathy," as Carl R. Rogers puts it (Rogers 1961), sends the message to our clients that we accept them, that they are not alone, and that it is safe to open up. Children benefit enormously from our attempts to consider things from their point of view. They feel listened to, drop their defences, and are able to grow in positive ways. Rogers pioneered the study of psychotherapy, and a large body of research supports the effectiveness of therapist empathy.

Psychologist and empathy researcher Jamil Zaki speaks of tuning in to the emotional frequencies of others and being motivated to help (Zaki 2019). I try to walk in each child's shoes and to see things through their eyes. In *On Becoming a Person*, Rogers lists the questions that he asks himself to facilitate empathy, including, "Can I let myself enter fully into the world of his feelings and personal meanings and see these as he does?" (Rogers 1961, p. 53). Building on Rogers' questions, I find it helpful to ask myself the following questions: How can I begin to step into the child's shoes? How can I gently venture into their thoughts and feelings? How can I wander around—without losing myself—so that I can more deeply understand them? It is not always easy.

To give an example: one month into therapy, a 10-year-old client, Sienna, told me that she felt upset about being selected for the school volleyball team rather than the school netball team, which was her preference. "I am not doing any volleyball training sessions or games," she remarked with determination. "I'm not doing it." As I considered her words, I realised that there was something about her rigidity that was irritating to me. Sienna was generally unwilling to engage in the work of therapy, choosing instead to draw picture after picture of her pet rabbit. How should I proceed? How could I begin to empathise with her perspective? I paused and asked myself: Why is she feeling this way? What is she thinking? As I slowed down, I remembered that I too was not selected for my preferred sporting team in Year 5. I recalled my feelings of disappointment, confusion, and frustration. It did not seem fair. I remembered thinking that adults sometimes seemed to make decisions without considering my point of view.

"It can be so frustrating when teachers don't seem to understand what their students want," I said.

"Yes!" Sienna exclaimed. "It's so annoying."

Somewhere along the way Sienna had learned that it was not acceptable to make mistakes, and she was wary about attempting many activities because they felt scary. My job was not to push back against her resistance and objections and to try to make her conform, which would only increase her rigidity, but to calmly meet her where she was at without judgement. Helping her to be in touch with her own feelings allowed her to open up to herself and to other possibilities.

"But I guess it must be hard for the teachers when there are so many students who want to play netball," she said.

I feel strongly that child therapists must be in contact with their own childhood memories to be genuinely effective. If this is difficult, we can also seek to draw parallels with adult equivalent situations. An adult equivalent situation in Sienna's case would be getting turned down for a job. My attempts to peer into Sienna's inner world invariably led to a stronger bond between us. We are all human beings, and we were all children once. As you try to empathise with the feelings and experiences of your clients, I encourage you to stop for a moment, remember your own childhood, and listen sensitively and empathically to yourself so that you may listen sensitively and empathically to your clients.

3 Focus on Feelings

> But feelings can't be ignored, no matter how unjust or ungrateful they seem.
> Anne Frank, *The Diary of a Young Girl* (p. 153)
> (Frank 2019; originally published in 1947)

The word "feeling" is derived from the Old English word "felen" meaning to perceive by touch or physical sensation. Feelings happen inside of us, and we judge them as being pleasant or unpleasant. Children experience life with great intensity and feel things deeply. They can also feel overwhelmed easily. Perhaps this is because they are often experiencing events and situations for the first time and have no point of comparison. Everything is brand new. It might also be because they have not yet learned how to cope with their strong feelings.

We can help children to handle their feelings by helping them to acknowledge and to put words to their feelings. In their book, *The Whole-Brain Child*, child psychiatrist Daniel J. Siegel and psychotherapist Tina Payne Bryson use the phrase "name it to tame it" to describe the act of noticing and labelling feelings (Siegel and Bryson 2011, p. 27). When we say, "I feel angry" or "I'm feeling sad" it helps us to make sense of what is happening, which can help us to feel calmer. Other sayings about feelings include "feel it to heal it" and "what you resist, persists," which has been attributed to Carl G. Jung. Like all of us, children need to learn the skills of recognising and expressing feelings so that they don't get swept up or stuck in their feelings.

I believe that talking about feelings is one of our primary tasks as therapists and that feelings should be spoken about from the outset. In my first session with a child, I might say: "Everyone has feelings. We all feel happy, sad, angry, scared, excited, frustrated, bored, and embarrassed at times. We feel our feelings in our bodies. One way of knowing what we are feeling is to listen to our bodies. How do you know when you're feeling happy? What happens inside your body?" My aim is to help children to realise that we all have feelings and that we all experience different types of feelings. I like to use the *Feeling Faces* poster (Havighurst and Harley 2007) as we begin to talk about feelings. We might read through the feeling words together and act out the different feelings together.

Most children are familiar with carrying a backpack, and I often use a backpack metaphor when talking about feelings. I might say:

> Sometimes, we don't want to feel certain feelings because they can be tricky, and we might want to push those feelings away. Just imagine that your feelings are like rocks in a backpack. If you keep carrying that backpack without taking the rocks out it will weigh you down and it will be hard to move. But if you take the time to open the backpack and look at them, you will feel lighter, and you'll be able to focus on what matters.

My aim here is to help children to discover that they can talk about feelings openly and that getting in touch with and sharing their feelings can help them to release and resolve their feelings.

I often use *The Bears* (2022) or the *Reflexions* cards (2001) to invite children to identify and talk about their feelings. When using *The Bears*, I might say: "How are the different bears feeling?" "Using *The Bears*, how are you feeling now?" You could create your own set of cards. I like *The Bears* because they can be used with anyone, including very young children and teenagers, and people from all backgrounds. In my work, it is evident that different children express their feelings in different ways. Some children smile when they feel happy, whereas others smile when they feel angry. By being curious about each child's unique emotional world and by asking thoughtful questions about their feelings using resources like *The Bears* or the *Reflexions* cards, we can better understand and validate their feelings. I might ask: "Have you ever felt that way?" "What did you notice in your body when that was happening?".

A final word on this topic: we can easily fall into the trap of intellectualising our clients' experiences, as can our clients themselves. Our job as child therapists is to be tuned in to and focused on the feelings being expressed, including our clients' feelings in the moment and towards us: "You feel frustrated that it's time to finish up." When we work closely with and reflect each child's feelings, we send the message to our clients that they are seen, heard, understood, and accepted. One example: Leah was a 13-year-old girl who was referred to me after a year of cutting herself. During our time together, I had often inquired about her feelings.

In our final session, I asked, "What's something you learned about yourself during our sessions?"

"I'm more aware when I get anxious or sad or other feelings. And I feel ok about that," she replied.

"Was there a moment in counselling that you found especially helpful?" I asked.

"The cards with the feelings. It's easier to identify the feelings. It's like I have options."

By opening a window to Leah's feelings, she was able to begin to acknowledge, identify, and accept her feelings, and to accept herself. She was also able to release her feelings, which led to greater clarity about her situation.

4 Help Each Child to Relax

> ...inside of you, there is a peace and refuge, to which you can go at every hour of the day and be at home at yourself.
> Hermann Hesse, *Siddhartha* (p. 46)
> (Hesse 2020; originally published in 1922)

Children often carry feelings of stress in their bodies without even realising it. They have stomach aches, headaches, muscle tension, and sleeping difficulties. One 12-year-old client was so overcome with feelings of stress that he clenched his jaw and struggled to talk. He simply could not begin to express himself. I believe that teaching children the skills of relaxation helps them to feel calmer, to get in touch with their emotions, and to communicate what is driving their feelings of stress.

When teaching children how to relax, I find that using imagery helps. I came up with the following exercise myself, which is about climbing a tree. Most children like to climb trees. I grew up and now continue to live in the bush in the Dandenong Ranges. I remember very clearly climbing a wattle tree as a child and spending hours sitting in it, often reading. I remember experiencing deep feelings of calm and relaxation. This exercise was also inspired by *The Magic Faraway Tree Collection* by Enid Blyton, a series I enjoyed as a child and read to my three children (Blyton 2020; originally published in 1939–1946). I might say:

> Imagine that you are walking in the bush. You are welcome to close your eyes, or you might choose to cast your eyes downward. As you walk, take a few slow, deep breaths. As you continue to walk, notice what you can see, perhaps some small ferns near your feet or some bark peeling off a gum tree up ahead. Notice what you can hear, perhaps the singing of a magpie or a kookaburra calling. Notice what you can feel, perhaps the feel of the sun shining in your face or the soft earth under your feet. Notice what you can smell, perhaps the smell of the damp dirt or the scent of gum leaves. Up ahead, you see a tree that looks just right for climbing, tall with lots of strong branches. You walk to the tree and then slowly hoist yourself up onto the first branch and climb up, higher and higher. You keep climbing and climbing until you reach what seems to be the top of the tree. You see a small wooden door above your head, like an attic door. You pull it open, and you climb through it and enter what you know to be a calm and relaxing space. As you take your next breath in through your nose, you feel your breath flowing deep into your belly. As you breathe out, you feel all of the tension leaving your body. As you breathe in again, you notice a wave of relaxation washing over you, from the top of your head down to the tips of your toes. You look around this calm and relaxing space and you see all of the things that make you feel calm. They might be objects, people, sounds, colours. After you have spent some time in this space, I want you to slowly come back into this room. You might wriggle your fingers and your toes, and gradually open your eyes if you've had your eyes closed.

The experience of going on a peaceful journey and imagining a calm space is very soothing. Afterwards, I will often ask children to draw or paint their calm space: "Paint your calm space." "Tell me about your calm space." A nine-year-old girl, Evelyn, who struggled to regulate her emotions when overwhelmed said that: "My calm space has cushions all around and a few armchairs and a bookshelf and my dog because he helps me feel calmer. When he licks my hand, he makes me smile. The colours are pastel rainbows swirling around." Doing this exercise helped to bring calmness into her body. Jon Kabat-Zinn's *Mountain Meditation* is one of the most peaceful exercises I have come across (Kabat-Zinn 1994). This is my adaptation for children:

> Imagine the most beautiful mountain. Notice the shape of the mountain. Notice how massive it is. When you feel ready, imagine that you are the mountain. Your head is the peak of the mountain, your shoulders and arms are the sides of the mountain, and the lower half of your body is the base of the mountain. Imagine that your body is rooted in the earth, and like a mountain, is quiet and still. Imagine changes in the seasons, from summer, to autumn, to winter, to spring. Imagine changes in the weather, sometimes bright sunshine, sometimes pouring rain, and sometimes wild storms. Through it all, the mountain just sits. In our lives, we experience storms and sunshine, darkness and light, changing thoughts and feelings, joy and sadness. By becoming a mountain, we can feel stronger and more stable. Just like a mountain, we can be still, no matter what the weather is like in our lives. I invite you to carry the mountain image in your mind the next time you feel buffeted by the weather.

It's no coincidence that these two exercises are about the natural world. Nature is healing, and we feel more relaxed and at ease in natural environments. Researchers believe that just hearing natural sounds can induce feelings of relaxation (Jo, Song et al. 2019). Relaxation is also a skill that we can teach children. The more children practice, the more they can find their own "inner mountain" and access this inner stillness during moments of stress, freeing themselves to relate more fully to themselves and to others.

5 Provide Predictability

> ...the average child and, less obviously, the average adult in our society generally prefers a safe, orderly, predictable, lawful, organized world.
> Abraham Maslow, *Motivation and Personality* (p. 41)
> (Maslow 1970)

Children have limited control compared to adults. They typically do not have a choice about where they live or who they live with. They rely on their parents or caregivers for money and financial resources. While they might be asked about their preferences for clothing, social activities, and schooling, these decisions are ultimately made by their parents. A child's sense of control and security comes from predictable and stable routines. This was very apparent during the COVID-19 pandemic lockdowns, when many of us struggled with changes to our everyday routines. Children were particularly vulnerable to the unpredictability of the crisis, and they often craved the familiarity of their pre-pandemic lives. While some children felt happier during lockdowns, perhaps due to improved sleep, more time to exercise, and closer family relationships (Soneson, Puntis et al. 2023), most missed their regular school schedules and their friends terribly.

Many parents helped their children to find that sense of security again by providing regularity and stability to their days. They created new structures and a new order. In my family, we tried to have a daily routine of schoolwork in the morning and art, sport, and play in the afternoon so that my children knew what to expect. Consistent daily routines are essential for children's wellbeing because they provide a predictable structure that supports their personal growth and development (Hosokawa, Tomozawa and Katsura 2023). Like all of us, when children know what is coming next, they feel more in charge and better able to prepare themselves for what is ahead, which helps them to approach upcoming situations with less stress and greater optimism.

These principles of predictability are just as relevant and beneficial in the therapy room. Child therapists can give therapy a structure by having regular opening and closing routines. I like using Scott Miller's *Child Outcome Rating Scale* near the start of each session and his *Child Session Rating Scale* towards the end of each session (Miller and Duncan 2000, Miller, Duncan and Johnson 2000). These scales allow children to let me know how they are doing (the *Child Outcome Rating Scale*) and how they feel about our time together (the *Child Session Rating Scale*) in a quick and easy way. I might start a session with, "Last week, you let me know that things had been hard at home. How are things going in your family this week? Can you let me know how things are going in your family by putting a mark on this line?" My aim with these questions is twofold: to help give each session a structure and to know each child's point of need: "where should we begin?" (to reference a phrase commonly used by therapists). These scales also help me to more closely examine each child's progress and to work on becoming a more effective therapist. I welcome each child's feedback. Is our time together helping? Does the child think we are a good fit? I learn quite a lot about my clients and myself using these scales.

Children soon understand what usually happens in therapy, and this helps them to feel safe and free to open up, both about their feelings in general and about their feelings towards me. I find that children will generally remind me about the scales if I don't bring them up. They will also point out if I miss any of my other regular routines, such as offering them a glass of water: "Are you going to ask me if I want a glass of water?" Other helpful routines include inviting them to choose where they would like to sit, giving them a small notebook to write on, and walking them to the apartment verandah at the end of each session. My overall intent with all of these routines is to help my clients to feel stable and to promote greater expressiveness and togetherness. I compare these practices—which follow a typical order—to the rise and fall of the sun. Just as the sun rises and sets at a predictable time each day, so too is there a natural rhythm to our time together that my clients can depend on, helping them to feel calmer and more grounded. This is especially helpful for those children who feel apprehensive about therapy. This may seem obvious, but predictability does a lot to help such children to feel more confident about bringing things out into the open. Much like the dependable pattern of day and night, familiar routines provide a sense of comfort. You will find your own ways of providing comfort and familiarity to your clients.

CHAPTER 4

Deepening the Therapeutic Connection

1 Be Spontaneous

Such pure leaps and spirals –
Surely they travel
The world forever...
Sylvia Plath, *Ariel* (p. 27)
(Plath 1965)

Though we should support children to reveal more about themselves by providing predictability, we must also be spontaneous. This is because no two children are the same. Anyone who has more than one child or who has spent time with children will tell you that each child has their own way of being in the world. In his landmark book, *The Child, the Family, and the Outside World*, English paediatrician and child psychiatrist Donald W. Winnicott writes that "no two babies are alike" and implores mothers and fathers to trust their instincts and to get to know their individual babies so that they will be able to give them the specific help that they need (Winnicott 2021; originally published in 1957). Likewise, in her pioneering book, *Windows to Our Children*, Violet Oaklander writes

M. Andrews Luke, *A Guide to Relationship-Oriented Child Therapy*, Palgrave Texts in Counselling and Psychotherapy,
https://doi.org/10.1007/978-3-031-99658-0_4

that: "One must keep in mind that each child is a unique individual. No matter what particular technique is used, a good therapist stays with the process evolving with the child" (Oaklander 2007; originally published in 1978, p. 194). Oaklander's words are echoed by Irvin Yalom, who urges therapists to "be prepared to go wherever the patient goes" (Yalom 2002, p. 34).

My point in sharing these quotes is to emphasise that we must be willing to travel on an unstructured journey alongside our clients. Being flexible with our clients allows our clients to be their own unique selves during their time with us and allows us to develop a unique and trusting relationship with them which, by its very nature, becomes the catalyst for healing and growth. How to be spontaneous? I try to follow my own instincts. My words are unplanned and impromptu. I study my clients carefully and in detail so that I can be ready to adapt quickly to their changing needs. I try to embrace uncertainty and to be resourceful and creative. It is when I am creative that I am at my best.

Unfortunately, many therapists, particularly beginning therapists, are drawn to manualised therapies that follow a specific sequence of activities. This might be due to a lack of confidence. It might also be because healthcare systems and insurance companies often require therapists to judiciously follow standardised treatments that have been found to be effective in experimental settings. But a deep dependence on standardised treatment protocols can result in the therapist being overly rigid and losing sight of what matters most: the relationship between the therapist and the client.

I find that my clients are more likely to discover new things about themselves when I experiment and try out new methods. Take, for example, my work with Noah. He had been diagnosed with attention-deficit/hyperactivity disorder (ADHD) and a learning disorder, and his father reported that he "struggled with the emotions of things." In our second session, Noah asked to play Uno with me, but he quickly seemed confused by the rules of the game, and he said that he wanted to stop. As he looked out of the window, he told me that his favourite thing to do was to watch the sun set. I went with the flow, and I invited him to paint a sunset. Noah painted thoughtfully and meticulously, filling the whole page very carefully. I could sense that the most appropriate thing for me to do was to remain silent and to sit next to him and watch him as he worked. After Noah finished, I tried to ask in-the-moment questions that were just right for him given where he was at.

"What are you thinking about as you look at the sunset?" I asked.

"I'm thinking that it's hard to focus on my work when the other kids are talking. And people get annoyed at me when I can't concentrate and I fidget," he said quietly and stared at the painting.

"What else are you thinking" I asked.

"Sunsets are calm."

"How are you like a sunset?" I asked.

He shrugged. "I guess I can be calm," he said.

"I can see that right now," I said.

"Yeah," he said, his face cheering up.

I hadn't asked these specific questions or used these specific words with a client before, but by doing so and by being open and relaxed in my approach with Noah, he was able to give expression to the feelings he had and to have a better understanding of and appreciation for who he was. He could see that people were often irritated by his behaviour, and he felt bad about himself. By casually acknowledging the positive aspects of Noah as he sat opposite me, Noah also realised that he could feel proud of himself. I felt pleased with this interaction.

There are no blueprints for healing. No two children and no two therapy sessions with children are the same. Children are not machines. They are unique living and breathing beings, and they know themselves best, even if they can't always put it in words. We must listen to what they are conveying to us to guide our work rather than following a script. Good child therapy is ultimately a dance between predictability and unpredictability. One final note on this topic: it's important to recognise that being spontaneous means that we might stumble or step on each other's toes in the process. What is crucial is to continue working on the relationship and to devise a new dance for each child based on the unique needs and strengths of each child.

2 Explore the Therapeutic Relationship

> The meeting of two personalities is like the contact of two chemical substances: if there is any reaction, both are transformed.
> C. G. Jung, *Modern Man in Search of a Soul* (p. 57)
> (Jung 1933)

When writing about human relationships, Carl G. Jung used the analogy of two chemical substances coming together to describe what happens when two individuals meet and influence each other (Jung 1933). Jung also spoke of the therapist-client relationship as a good example of the transformative power of a close connection between two people. Our clients are shaped by our encounters and interactions with them, and we are shaped by our encounters and interactions with our clients.

Research has confirmed what many therapists have known all along: that the therapeutic relationship is essential for helping our clients to heal. Indeed, an American Psychological Association (APA) task force found that:

> The psychotherapy relationship makes substantial and consistent contributions to outcome independent of the type of treatment. Decades of research evidence and clinical experience converge: The relationship works! These effect sizes concretely translate into healthier and happier people. (Norcross and Lambert 2018, p. 313)

At its heart, therapy is a human relationship, and we therapists bring our own selves into every therapy session. The best therapists take the time to nurture their relationships with their clients, and they make the care and cultivation of each relationship their highest priority. Psychotherapy researcher Charles Gelso and his collaborators describe the therapeutic relationship as being made up of a "working alliance" (the establishment of a working bond); a "transference/countertransference configuration" (the influence of earlier relationships on the perceptions of the client and the therapist towards one another); and a "real relationship" (how the client and therapist see each other) (Hill, An et al. 2024). I often ask myself: How does my client see me? Do they see me as a trustworthy person? What can I do to help them to feel safe enough to reveal who they are to me? I also ask myself: How do I see my client? What can I do to see them more clearly and to understand them better?

I always try to tune in to, honour, and respect each client's cultural identity, including their values, traditions, and beliefs, perhaps by saying: "Tell me more about yourself." I want to learn more so that I can strengthen our therapeutic relationship.

I make a point of speaking about the therapeutic relationship with my clients directly, and I regularly ask my clients: "How are we going today?" or "How are you and I going?" For some therapists, the thought of explicitly checking in with their clients about their experiences of the therapeutic relationship is anxiety-provoking. To my mind, directly asking our clients about their experiences is a vital ingredient of effective therapy.

I routinely monitor each client's experience of our relationship by inviting them to use rating scales to let me know their opinion of me and how we are working. Recall my earlier comments about using Scott Miller's *Child Session Rating Scale* towards the end of each session (Miller and Duncan 2000; Miller et al., 2000). At the end of the initial session, I might say softly:

> Remember at the start of our time together today I explained that my job is to work together with you and to build a good relationship. Remember I said that that I would ask you how *we* are going. Sometimes the children I see find it easier to let me know how we are going by putting marks on the lines on this piece of paper. Do you feel like I listened to you today? Did you like what we did today? How much out of 10? Let me know how you feel by putting a mark on these lines.

Checking in directly helps me to better understand what is working and what is not and to make any adjustments to better meet each child's needs. It can feel daunting for children to give feedback, but I find that asking these questions in a gentle way invariably invigorates our relationship and our time together.

One boy, Isaiah, aged nine, marked me as 6 out of 10 for listening in our second session. Initially, embarrassed feelings came up for me. I then told him that his assessment was accurate, and I apologised. I had not been fully present with him, and I had found myself getting lost in thoughts of a project I was due to complete later that day. Together, we talked about my lack of concentration and how I could do better next time. He became animated when he shared his thoughts, and our exchange helped to bring me back, and to put our relationship back on track. My open acknowledgement of my failure to listen well sent Isaiah the message that he was important to me, and proved to be beneficial for him. Isaiah came to realise the value of sharing his feelings and later did a drawing for his Dad, a shift worker who was often absent, that conveyed how much he missed him. More often than not the experience of exploring the therapeutic relationship honestly is illuminating for our clients.

3 Encourage Awareness Through Play

> …to 'play it out' is the most natural self-healing measure childhood affords.
> Erik Erikson, *Childhood and Society* (p. 200)
> (Erikson 1987; originally published in 1950)

Playing is the way that children make sense of their lives. Through play, children learn about themselves and how the world works. Play is critical for children's cognitive, emotional, physical, and social development and mental health. It allows children to explore their experiences, and to test out different ways of behaving. Children have an innate desire to play, and play helps them to master the skills they will need as adults, such as problem-solving, creativity, independence, and social skills. Play is so important that it is recognised as a fundamental right of every child under the United Nations Declaration on the Rights of the Child (Article 31).

Despite this, adults often trivialise children's play and underestimate the benefits. For many children today, a lot of their leisure time is spent in front of a screen or participating in adult-directed, structured, and risk-averse activities. Play researchers Helen Dodd and Kathryn Lester write that when children do not have the opportunity to play in an adventurous way—and experience the accompanying feelings of excitement, thrill, and fear—they do not get the opportunity to learn about heightened physical states, uncertainty, and coping, and are likely to struggle with feelings of anxiety (Dodd and Lester 2021). To play is to learn how to navigate uncomfortable feelings and to cope in healthy ways. As Donald W. Winnicott puts it, "children play to master anxiety" (Winnicott 2021; originally published in 1957, p. 135).

The use of play in therapy has a long history. In the early twentieth century, the first practicing child psychoanalyst, Hermine Hug-Hellmuth, recognised play as a window to children's inner lives (Plastow 2011). Melanie Klein, the Austrian psychoanalyst, observed in the 1920s that children expressed their fears and other feelings through their play and introduced the concept of the "play technique," which involved interpreting children's play: "all Klein had to do to learn of the child's overarching anxieties, defences, and inhibitions was watch the child's play" (Britzman 2016). More than 70 years ago, Virginia Axline, an influential American psychologist and play therapist, invited children to describe their experiences of play therapy, and concluded that play therapy helped to reduce the "sharp edges" of feelings and helped children to "(sharpen) their awareness of themselves" (Axline 1950, p. 62). Since the publication of her groundbreaking book, *Play Therapy*, which outlines her basic principles of play therapy, such as not attempting to direct, steer, or influence the child's play, communication, or behaviour, many child therapists have embraced her non-directive approach (Axline 1990; originally published in 1947).

In my own work with children, I assume a somewhat more directive approach. I provide children with a selection of play materials, including art supplies, miniature animals, and games. I watch how they play. Are they gentle in their movements? Are they rushed? I comment on what is happening: "You're not sure where to start." "You like working carefully." "The animals are all together." I watch for patterns. Are there themes of death and dying? Nurturing? Power? Self-doubt? Problem-solving and mastery? Danger? Later on, I become more directive, and I ask specific questions: "Do you feel scared sometimes?" "What are you thinking?" "What does this remind you of?" I follow the child's lead, and I make suggestions. That's part of the dance of child therapy.

How each child plays is very telling. Their play is honest and candid, and I learn a lot about their innermost feelings and beliefs, and how they relate to the world and others. In contrast to adults, who "talk out" their feelings, children "play out" their feelings. Take 11-year-old Jacob. He was brought in to see me because he had a problem with his peers. He had few friends and his behaviour often alienated others. He examined my shelf and took down the Jenga game. He self-consciously built a tower and nodded at me to play with him. We played three games in a row.

I asked, "Does playing Jenga remind you of anything?"

He said, "Sometimes when they are mean to me it's like a piece of me coming out, like Jenga. And you've got to make sure it doesn't topple over, you don't fall, break under pressure."

Playing Jenga made it easier for Jacob to express some difficult things about himself: he felt hurt and rejected and had constructed a protective wall around himself. My role was to listen and acknowledge his feelings of rejection in a calm manner. By demonstrating that I allowed and accepted his feelings and took him seriously, Jacob was able to more fully explore his feelings, to feel less alone in his feelings, and to gain greater mastery over his feelings. As he left my office, he smiled and said, "You know what, it's actually not that bad. Caleb likes to hang out with me on the playground. I'm going to his house on the weekend." He seemed lighter. This was a good example of a child learning that the world was not such a bad place and that it was safe to be himself. He realised that he no longer had to retreat behind his protective wall.

4 Invite Children to Draw

> Children who are not able to talk about their wishes and needs in connection with past, present and future situations may be able to do so by using the symbolic language of drawing.
> Kathryn Gelderd, David Geldard, and Rebecca Yin Foo, *Counselling Children* (p. 226)
> (Geldard, Geldard and Foo 2018; originally published in 1997)

Drawing is one of the oldest methods of human communication. It helps people to express themselves. It is often fun and energising. It can also be calming. The physical act of drawing can be meditative and allow us to be more fully in the present moment. Hungarian psychologist Mihaly Csikszentmihalyi says that drawing can produce a flow state, or the experience of being completely immersed in a task (Csikszentmihalyi 2002; originally published in 1992). My oldest daughter is an artist and can spend days drawing. She seems to be totally absorbed when she is drawing and everything else falls away.

Flow has been linked with creativity, positive feelings, and enhanced wellbeing (Csikszentmihalyi 1997, Rogatko 2009). Csikszentmihalyi says that: "Whenever the goal is to improve the quality of life, flow theory can point the way" (Csikszentmihalyi 2002; originally published in 1992, p. 5). A study by art therapy researcher Seung Yeon Lee found that Korean immigrant children who were having challenges adapting to their new home were better able to cope with their struggles and more likely to experience feelings of enjoyment after engaging in art-making activities such as drawing (Lee 2013). Drawing researchers Jennifer Drake and

Ellen Winner write that when children are able to freely construct drawings from their own imagination—rather than simply copying existing images—their mood improves (Drake and Winner 2013).

I have encountered this in my work with children. Almost all children take pleasure in drawing, but they seem to respond more enthusiastically when they have the freedom to create an entirely new drawing, rather than using structured drawing worksheets, presumably because this allows them to be more in control of what they draw and is sufficiently challenging. I might invite children to draw how they are feeling or to draw their day. "Draw what's been happening today." "Draw a picture of your sadness."

I find it most helpful to ask children to draw their families and the people who populate their lives: "Draw the people in your life." In *Windows to Our Children*, there are many examples of wonderful drawing prompts, including: "Close your eyes and go into your space. Now think of each member of your family. If you were to draw them on a piece of paper as something they remind you of, what would that be?" (Oaklander 2007; originally published in 1978). Drawings of family are revealing, and they deepen the work.

Remember Isaiah, aged nine, who missed his Dad. He had been referred to me because of frequent meltdowns at home. His parents commented that he was, "very uncooperative recently, and throws tantrums and screams." In Isaiah's first session with me, I invited him to draw his family. This is what he said about his drawing: "I'm like my Dad. We both like the colour blue. I like to do things with my Dad. I feel sad about not seeing my Dad. My Dad works a lot. His work hours have changed. I only see him two days a week." His eyes filled with tears. It was clear to me that he had been using all of his energy to hold in his feelings of sadness and despair about his Dad's absences, and that those feelings had been erupting ever since. With Isaiah's permission, I told his parents about our time together. Isaiah's words about his Dad and his drawings threw light on his behaviour at home. With this new understanding, Isaiah's Dad made an effort to spend more time with him.

At the next session, I asked Isaiah to draw an animal and to tell me how he was like the animal. He drew a lion. He looked at me and said, "I am brave." Drawing made it easier for Isaiah to discover and express his feelings about what was going on and to cope with his feelings. Drawing also gave him a sense of accomplishment. Look at what I can do and what I have created. I usually invite children to take their drawings home.

Before they leave, I scan their drawings. We often revisit their drawings at the end of our sessions. This is a valuable exercise. Children are always fascinated to see how far they have come.

5 Paint

> Painting is self-discovery. Every good artist paints what he is.
> Jackson Pollock

Children love painting. They enjoy the tactile experience of smearing and mixing the paints and creating new colours. Paint oozes, gushes, and spurts. The sweeping motions of painting can be soothing. Swishing the water in the paintbrush cup can also be relaxing. For many children, the very act of painting and washing their brush is more enjoyable for them than the final product.

When children paint, there is a continuous interchange between their ideas, thoughts, and feelings and the specific surfaces, brushes, and paints used, each influencing the other. Oil paint is thick and rich. Acrylic paint is smooth, light, and vibrant. Watercolours are translucent and luminous. I often use watercolour paints in my work with children because they are highly blendable and fast drying. They also come in trays, making them easy to take outside. I have thick construction paper for painting on and butcher's paper for finger painting. Finger painting is good for children who are frightened of making mistakes and cautious. I also have a supply of lightweight wooden stick people, which can be painted. Painting the stick people is another way of exploring the people who populate each child's life.

The process of painting is a way for children to develop a sense of who they are, and it helps them to develop a healthy view of themselves. I might say: "Paint yourself as a baby." "Paint yourself when you are happy." "Paint yourself when you are worried." "Tell me about your painting." "What does red/yellow/blue mean to you?" It might seem too abstract for children to identify what specific colours mean to them, but most children can do it and are excited to be asked. "Red is my love." "Yellow is when I am warm and cosy." "Blue is when I am sad and blue."

Remember six-year-old Emma whose Mum had died unexpectedly. I invited Emma to paint some wooden stick people and to make each figure represent a different person in her life. I often work with children when they paint, and I joined her. We dripped and dabbed the paint on our first figures. At first, Emma painted smiling faces only on her figures.

"This is my Gran when she talks with me," she said.

I had a hunch that it might be helpful to change it up and I wondered out loud about painting different types of facial expressions: "Only smiling faces? No other faces?"

Emma asked, "Can I paint a dead face?"

"Yes," I said softly.

"A dead face means what my Mum had," she explained. "This is my Mum. Does your Mum have a dead face?" she asked.

"No," I said gently. "My Mum is still alive."

"That's unfair," she said, as she painted black lines for eyes on the figure of her Mum.

"What are you feeling now, Emma?" I asked.

"I feel angry," she said.

This session reminded me of two things. First, many adults are scared to discuss death with children. This might be because it makes them feel anxious or because they worry about saying the wrong thing. Welcoming Emma's request to paint "a dead face" sent Emma the message that death is not too awful to talk about, and it allowed Emma to sharpen her sense of who she is: someone who can cope with her Mum's death. Second, with the right conditions, children will always take us where they need to go. Painting helped Emma to begin to acknowledge and feel her feelings about her Mum's death, including her fury at the unjustness of it all, and to share her story. The paint flows, and the child's story begins.

CHAPTER 5

Additional Creative Techniques

1 Use Clay

Time past and time future
What might have been and what has been
Point to one end, which is always present.
T.S. Eliot, *The Four Quartets* (p. 14)
(Eliot 2019; originally published in 1943)

A great many of my clients are not in the here-and-now. They are caught up in painful episodes from the past or worriedly anticipating future events: "Something bad is going to happen." "What if?" There is something about the physicality of clay that allows children to more clearly see, know, and face their worries and to reconnect with themselves in the current moment. Clay is thick, damp, cold, and easily moulded. Children instinctively want to touch clay and explore it. Manipulating clay helps children to focus and concentrate. It is relaxing, and it helps children to feel grounded as they work.

The defining feature of clay is its flexibility when wet. Children can work it with their palms, knead it, pinch it, prod it, tear it, and smooth it. I have a large sheet of plywood, which is a good surface to work on. It can be wiped clean easily before and after working on it. There is a sink in the apartment that can be used to wash hands. We can work with

M. Andrews Luke, *A Guide to Relationship-Oriented Child Therapy*, Palgrave Texts in Counselling and Psychotherapy,
https://doi.org/10.1007/978-3-031-99658-0_5

clay in my office or outside on the verandah. Sometimes I ask children to make themselves when they were a baby or to make themselves now or to make themselves how they want to be. Sometimes I ask them to make their family or friends. Other times I ask them to make their fears.

A 13-year-old girl, Abigail, was afraid of an upcoming flight: "There's no way I'm getting on that plane." I placed a lump of clay between us. Abigail squeezed the clay and rubbed it between her fingers. I asked Abigail to make a plane with the clay. I observed her carefully as she continued to fiddle with the clay. She was reluctant to start. She frowned and looked down. "I don't know if I can do it." Her hesitation was revealing. I gently offered to make my own plane alongside her. She cautiously copied my movements. Gradually, she became absorbed in making her own plane.

"How are you feeling about flying?" I asked after some time.

Abigail grimaced. "Worried. Apprehensive. Embarrassed," she sighed.

"Tell me more," I said.

"I might not be able to do this. People might judge me negatively," she said as she continued to shape her clay.

Abigail cried. She had a low opinion of herself. She felt different. She had been criticised and ridiculed by the adults in her world about her general reluctance to tackle new situations, and she found it hard to accept herself, including her feelings. The act of working the clay helped Abigail to feel calm enough to hold her feelings in awareness and move through her distress. It helped her to watch her feelings without being drawn into them and to learn that she did not have to be a prisoner of her anxiety about the past or her fears of the future. Clay reminds us that we are here now.

2 Use Animals

> Animals are such agreeable friends – they ask no questions, they pass no criticism.
> George Eliot, *Scenes of Clerical Life* (p. 137)
> (Eliot 1857/n.d.)

Almost all children love animals. Children are drawn to books about animals, movies with animal characters, toy animals, and live animals.

Children are naturally curious, and they are captivated by the interesting appearance, behaviour, and sounds of animals. Child development researcher Judy S. DeLoache and her colleagues have noted that babies as young as four months much prefer animals over inanimate objects (DeLoache, Pickard and LoBue 2011). Babies smile, laugh, and wave at animals. DeLoache writes that humans have likely evolved to be fascinated by animals from a young age because detecting, understanding, and interacting with animals is crucial for human survival and benefited our ancestors. It's no surprise that young children bond quickly and easily with animals and pets and that pet ownership in homes with children is high. Indeed, a study of pet ownership in Australia found that 86% of Australian homes with children have pets (Australia 2022).

Child therapists can harness children's innate love of animals. They can use animals in therapy to develop rapport with children and to explore each child's relationships and ways of relating. The use of animals in therapy includes using stuffed toy animals, toy animal puppets, and miniature animals, and working with therapy animals. In my work, I find it helpful to use realistic looking miniature animals and to make animal puppets with my clients. I have a wooden bowl that contains about 30 miniature animals, including farm animals, wild animals, dinosaurs, and reptiles. I also use cardboard craft cylinders to make animal puppets with my clients. Children find it much easier to act out their stories using animals than to share what they are feeling directly. I find that teenagers often like using miniature animals as well. My task is to help each client to share the stories of their relationships and to identify key themes. I might begin by asking: "Which animal is most like you? Why?" "Which animals are most like your family members? Why?" "Tell a story about the animals."

Recall Emma, whose Mum had died unexpectedly. A couple of days before we were due to meet, Emma had experienced a very difficult morning. Her grandmother explained to me that she had woken up in the early hours of the morning upset because she wanted to speak to her Mum one last time.

In therapy, I placed the bowl of miniature animals between us, and I invited Emma to choose an animal that was most like her.

Emma sighed, "You don't have the right animal. I'm like a lovebird. A bird that can fly."

"What about your Mum? Which animal is most like your Mum?" I asked.

"My Mum is a lovebird as well," she said.

I didn't have any lovebirds, so I did a Google image search of "lovebirds." I then asked Emma to choose the ones that were most like herself and her Mum. Emma chose a blue lovebird to represent herself and a yellow lovebird to represent her Mum. I printed the images, and we stuck them on cardboard cylinders.

"Tell me about the lovebirds," I asked.

"Lovebirds are a pair," she explained.

Emma then picked up the two lovebirds and moved them in unison above the other miniature animals.

"What might the yellow lovebird like to say to the blue lovebird?" I asked.

"I just like to fly to be with you and to avoid those predators down below," she said.

"I wonder what the blue lovebird might like to say to the yellow lovebird," I asked.

"We are going on an adventure. You can bring a friend. Bring another fellow bird with you. Like an ostrich or an owl. Then we will be ready to go on an adventure," she said.

Later, I asked, "What are the lovebirds thinking?"

"They love each other. They are thinking about cuddling. They're leaning into each other. It's like me and my Mum," she said softly.

"The lovebirds love each other very much," I said gently. Emma nodded, and her eyes were filled with joy.

I learned a lot about Emma that day. I was deeply moved by the expressions of affection between the lovebirds, and what they revealed about Emma's relationship with her Mum. The use of animals was very therapeutic for Emma. It helped ease some of her anguish about losing her Mum. The word "animal" comes from the Latin word "animalis," which means "having breath" or "having a soul." Using animals helped Emma to bring the loving bond she had with her Mum to life.

3 Read Books Together

Books are the mirrors of the soul.
Virginia Woolf, *Between the Acts* (p. 13)
(Woolf 2022; originally published in 1941)

I use books to talk with children about their feelings and situations. Most young children like to have story books read to them. I find that teenagers enjoy story books as well. Children and young people can relate to the experiences of the characters. Books can also open children up to new perspectives and possibilities. Books with repetitive, rhythmic language can be soothing. I often read books in my first couple of sessions with my clients. The act of reading books together helps to create a bond between myself and my clients.

Students often ask me which books to use in therapy. Over the years, I have built up a careful selection of go-to books. I use *Little Red Riding Hood* (Grimm and Grimm 2012; originally published in 1812) to explore children's fears and feelings of helplessness: "Have you ever felt that way?" *Where The Wild Things Are* (Sendek 2000; originally published in 1963), *Alexander and the Terrible, Horrible, No Good, Very Bad Day* (Viorst 1986; originally published in 1972), and *The Very Cranky Bear* (Bland 2008) can be useful to explore anger. *The Giving Tree* (Silverstein 1992; originally published in 1964) opens up conversations about love and generosity. *Owl Moon* (Yolen 1987) is about a child who goes owling at night and opens up conversations about courage, patience, hope, and nature. I might ask: "Are you like any of the characters? In what way?"

Possum Magic (Fox 2008; originally published in 1983) is about a possum who becomes invisible and invites discussions about wishes and superpowers: "What would you do if you could become invisible?" "If you could have any superpower, what would it be?" *Herbert & Harry* (Allen 2000; originally published in 1986) is about conflict. *The Invisible String* (Karst 2000) is a beautiful book about separation, loss, and grief. *The Huge Bag of Worries* (Ironside 2004) is about a girl who accumulates more and more worries. *Ten Little Fingers and Ten Little Toes* (Fox 2008) prompts conversations about being a baby: "What were you like as a baby?" All of these books highlight, in their own way, the importance of relationships, support, and care. I might ask: "Who cares for you?" "Who do you care for?"

I have noticed an increasing number of children's books that are designed to explicitly teach children about feelings. I find that children don't usually like these books. These books, while well intentioned, often come across as contrived. The best books tell a story and are open to interpretation. Think about the books you loved as a child. Why did you love them? The most thoughtful books help to give voice to our clients' experiences and bring us closer together.

4 Encourage Mindful Movements

> One of the clearest lessons from contemporary neuroscience is that our sense of ourselves in anchored in a vital connection with our bodies. We do not truly know ourselves unless we can feel and interpret our physical sensations; we need to register and act on these sensations to navigate safely through life.
> Bessel van der Kolk, *The Body Keeps the Score* (p. 272)
> (van der Kolk 2015; originally published in 2014)

A great number of the children I work with are out of synch with their bodily sensations and feelings. Perhaps this is because they have experienced difficult or traumatic events, and disconnecting from their emotions and bodily sensations is a way of protecting themselves from their pain. Contrast this with young babies, who are attuned to their bodies and who feel and express their feelings immediately and without a filter. I have tender memories of my now 10-year-old son taking great delight in his own movements as a baby, such as getting up on all fours and rocking backwards and forwards. He was—and continues to be—skilled at moving and sensing his body. His pleasure comes from simply doing what comes naturally and from using his body expressively, especially when he plays sport.

The inability of some children to attend to the flow of sensations and signals arising in their bodies—also known as interoception signals—might also be linked to children's frequent use of digital devices. A large study showed that 8- to 12-year-olds spend 5½ hours each day on devices for non-school related activities and that 13- to 18-year-olds spend even more time on devices outside of schoolwork, averaging 8½ hours each day (Rideout, Peebles et al. 2022). Although digital technologies can have benefits, such as providing children with access to social supports,

I believe that spending too much time using digital devices contributes to a sense of detachment. How can we help children to better notice and tolerate what is going on inside themselves? How can we help them to reestablish their bodily awareness, which leads to a better connection with themselves and with others? I have found that encouraging children to engage in mindful movements—deliberate, controlled movements—can help enormously.

The most common sequence of movements I use in my therapy sessions is a yoga sequence known as Tadasana Urdhva Hastasana or Volcano Pose. I have been practicing yoga for a long time, and this yoga sequence is very calming. I usually start by asking children to stand with their feet close together and to take a breath in:

> Take a deep breath. Imagine that you are a volcano. Follow my movements. Press your hands together in front of your heart. As you exhale, push your shoulders back and down. As you inhale, reach your arms up slowly, like a volcano gently erupting, look up, and bring your hands together above your head. As you exhale, bring your hands down together, palms touching, until they have returned to your heart, the lava flowing softly down the mountain.

We might repeat this sequence for a few minutes. As we go through the movements, I encourage children to observe what is happening in their body. "Become aware of your feet on the floor, like the base of a mountain grounded in the earth. Feel the weight of your body on your feet. Notice your breathing."

Another yoga sequence that works well with children is Vrksasana or Tree Pose. I might say:

> Take a deep breath. Take a look out the window at that big elm tree. Imagine that you are a tree. Imagine that your feet are the roots of the tree, growing deeply into the ground. Imagine that your arms are the branches of the tree and reach them out wide. Sway gently left and right, just like a tree in the breeze. If it feels right, gently lift one foot and rest the sole of that foot against the calf of your other leg.

Mirroring is sometimes useful. I might say: "Let's stand facing each other. I'm going to be the leader and you're the mirror. Copy my movements as closely as you can. Now let's swap and you be the leader."

Some children can find it difficult to stand in one spot. If that's the case, we might do a walking meditation. This can be done inside or outside. We might do a few loops of my office or walk on the grass outside. If it's a nice day, we might take our shoes off. Five minutes is a good amount of time. I might say: "Notice how your feet feel as you walk. Notice how your legs feel. Notice how your whole body feels. If your mind starts to wander, which it will, gently bring it back to how your body is feeling while we walk."

All of these movements remind children that they are in their bodies. They provide the means for each child to bring their attention back to their physical body and to recognise, understand, and regulate their emotions. As Dutch psychiatrist and writer Bessel van der Kolk writes: "Simply noticing what you feel fosters emotional regulation, and it helps you to stop trying to ignore what is going on inside of you" (p. 273). Mindful movements help children to relearn how to live inside their bodies and to feel comfortable.

A note of caution: although encouraging children to engage in mindful movements can help them to regulate and control their emotions, it can also exacerbate feelings of stress, particularly for those living with trauma. I have experienced this firsthand. Years ago, I tore my vertebral artery at the base of my brain while exercising and subsequently had two strokes. I lost sensation in the left side of my face and my right leg, and I had to learn how to walk again. When I returned to my yoga practice some months later and paid close attention to my legs felt I felt vulnerable, and my heart pounded. All I could remember in that moment were the minutes after the second stroke when I realised that my legs weren't working and that I could not walk. My body responded with alarm. In his book, *Trauma-Sensitive Mindfulness*, David Treleaven suggests that therapists can help their clients to stay within their "window of tolerance" by purposefully slowing the pace of the mindfulness practice, perhaps by engaging in shorter practice periods, or by encouraging clients to open their eyes, to take a few deep breaths, and to take breaks (Treleaven 2018).

Gradually, the mindful movements of yoga were healing for me. I took it one day at a time and slowly increased my time spent practicing. Gently observing my physical sensations helped me to learn that I could tune into my body again without fear, to feel safe in my body, and to feel stronger. We are embodied creatures. Mindful movements help children to listen to their bodies, to know how they are feeling, and to be in synch with themselves and others. They carry them back into the language of their bodies.

5 Share Stories of Hope

'Hope' is the thing with feathers –
That perches in the soul –
And sings the tune without the words –
And never stops – at all –
Emily Dickinson, *The Complete Poems of Emily Dickinson* (p. 116)
(Dickinson 1960)

Every day, we therapists hear the most intimate stories. Our clients share profoundly private details about their lives and fears. Being entrusted with such personal information is an incredible privilege. After my clients have left a session, I often think to myself: I am the first person to bear witness to that particular story. It never fails to amaze me: what an immense honour it is to be privy to such deeply held stories of struggle and perseverance. Each story might be different, but each story invariably reminds me of other clients' experiences or my own experiences. This is because we are all human, and we all have the same longing to be accepted by others, the same insecurities, and the same drive to search for light and meaning.

While recognising that we have an ethical duty to maintain confidentiality, I believe that we have a responsibility to carefully share stories and to emphasise the universality of feelings and challenges. Our clients might feel all alone in their fears, but they are ultimately not alone in their worries. I might say, for example: "I see lots of children your age. Many tell me that they too feel scared about making mistakes. They say that they get butterflies in their stomachs and that their muscles feel tense." Sharing the experiences of other children provides perspective and can be immensely reassuring for our clients.

I might also disclose personal information about myself if I have had a similar experience and I think it would benefit my client. One 16-year-old client, Sameera, had endured bullying from her former classmates at her previous school and felt anxious and worried about not being good enough: "I always think I'm a bad person. I feel like I'm being judged." When I asked her to tell me more about her worries, she explained:

"There's a block that stops me from doing a lot of things. Like public speaking. Like last Wednesday my friends said I should go for Sports Captain and make a speech. I hadn't prepared anything. I did not want to do it, so I didn't."

She was terrified at the prospect of speaking in public in front of her new friends with no preparation: "What if I had made a mistake and embarrassed myself?"

I responded by saying that many people fear public speaking more than death and that I had suffered through public speaking with a shaky voice. I shared that I had recently spoken at a national conference and that I had felt nervous at the prospect of the question-and-answer session after the presentation: what if people asked difficult questions and I blanked on key details? I also shared a quote widely attributed to Mark Twain about public speaking: "There are two types of speakers: those who are nervous and those who are liars."

I added: "Anxiety is hard. It can be exhausting. Other young people I've worked with have told me that certain things help. Things like just being with the people who care about them. Or certain breathing techniques. I have found these things to be helpful myself."

Her eyes lit up, and she looked pleasantly surprised. Telling her about my similar feelings of nervousness and possible ways of coping helped to alleviate her feelings of aloneness and shame and to be less critical of herself. Her struggles were part of the human condition. It was a joy to see her eyes grow wide with the thought of what might be: *maybe everything will be ok.*

A final point: we therapists can help our clients by sharing stories of hope and courage and by offering suggestions, but ultimately it is our care and concern that leads to the greatest personal growth and healing. Recall, for one last time, Emma, whose mother died unexpectedly. Emma listened intently whenever I shared stories of other children whose parents had died. These stories helped her to realise that she was not the only one and instilled a sense of hope. Nevertheless, it was my acts of kindness that were the most powerful. I met regularly with her grandparents, who were her main carers, and often asked how they regarded my work with Emma. During one of our final meetings, I invited them to share what they believed had helped Emma the most in therapy. Her grandmother explained that: "You made sure to always have her favourite art supplies on hand. You gave her your full attention. That made her feel good." Once again, what lingers is the human element, not words of advice or particular therapy techniques. My humanness was what had helped Emma the most.

CHAPTER 6

Nurturing Coping Skills and Empathy

1 Teach the Language of Coping

> Coping language provides the tools for conversations that can be had to facilitate reflection and growth.
> Erica Frydenberg, *Adolescent Coping* (p. 163)
> (Frydenberg 2018)

One of our major tasks as therapists is to help children to cope with stress. We can tell stories that offer hope and solutions. We can teach relaxation skills and support children to release their feelings. We can encourage mindful movements and play.

Sometimes I talk about what stress and coping are: "Stress is the feeling you get when something seems difficult or overwhelming. It's when your body is getting ready to respond to something challenging. You might feel tense or shaky. Coping is all of the things you can do to deal with feelings of stress. There are lots of different things you can do to deal with feelings of stress. Some things are helpful, and some things are less helpful." In this description I introduce a few key ideas: stress lives in our bodies; there are many different ways of coping with stress; and different ways of coping can be more or less effective.

Two excellent tools that can be used to support conversations with children and young people about their coping strategies are the *Early*

M. Andrews Luke, *A Guide to Relationship-Oriented Child Therapy*, Palgrave Texts in Counselling and Psychotherapy,
https://doi.org/10.1007/978-3-031-99658-0_6

Years Coping Cards (Frydenberg and Deans 2011) and the *Adolescent Coping Scale* (Frydenberg and Lewis 2011). They were developed by my mentor, Erica Frydenberg. The *Early Years Coping Cards* are a set of cards with pictures of everyday challenging situations for children, such as saying goodbye to a parent and being in the dark, and coping strategies, such as seeking comfort and crying. They can be used when working with pre- and primary-school aged children. I have found that children are always able to articulate how they manage different situations, and I always learn so many new things about them when using these cards.

The *Adolescent Coping Scale* is made up of a series of coping statements. It is one of my most useful instruments for working with teenagers. I sit next to my clients and read out the statements, which include, "Talk to others and give each other support," "Work hard," and "Criticise myself." I might say: "This is a list of different ways of coping. As I read them out, let me know how often you use them to cope with your concerns, from never and seldom through to often and very often." I often ask them to elaborate on their responses—"tell me more"—and I scribble down their answers in the margins. These answers generate a lot of information for later discussions.

When we have finished, we then score and review their coping strategies together. I might say: "Looking at your coping profile, it looks like the coping strategies you use most often are doing something relaxing and ignoring whatever is bothering you. Does this fit with what you know about yourself?" Young people are regularly asked to complete tests, including academic and diagnostic tests, and they are often anxious about them. In most situations, they do not see the test results and are not asked if they agree with the results. My main aim, of course, when asking my clients if they agree with the results is to send the message that I respect them and their ability to assess their own situation. A secondary aim is to deepen our follow-up conversations.

An example: Lily, a 15-year-old girl, was referred to me after the unexpected death of her father. Every time I mentioned her father and asked her how she felt, she shrugged. In our fourth session, I invited Lily to complete the *Adolescent Coping Scale*. She agreed with the results, which suggested that her main ways of coping included keeping fit, working hard, and focusing on the positive.

"Is that how you see yourself?" I asked.

"Yes, that's me," she said softly. "I focus on the positive. I just don't cry."

Lily's answer to my question shed much light on her situation and led to a cascade of pent-up feelings of grief and concern in later sessions about causing her family more feelings of unhappiness if she were to express her feelings openly. Completing the questionnaire and reflecting on her habitual ways of coping helped Lily to see herself more vividly and to be receptive to the idea of being more open with her feelings.

Another example involves Daniel, also aged 15, who was referred for therapy by his parents. They explained that, "Daniel is super smart but doesn't apply himself. At home he spends most of his time in his room with the computer. We're worried about his mental state. It's been building." In my first session with Daniel, he said, "I feel sad. I can't work out why. I want to feel happier and more motivated." His subsequent answers to the *Adolescent Coping Scale* suggested that his main ways of coping were playing sport, being funny, keeping things to himself, and ignoring his problems. When I asked him what he might like to do more or less often, he immediately responded by saying forcefully, "I want to stop keeping things to myself. I want to talk to other people more. I want to talk to my closest friends more." Daniel was using the language of coping in our first session. Encouraging Daniel to complete the questionnaire and our ensuing conversation proved meaningful, and together we worked out a schedule for talking and texting with his closest friends over the next few days.

By exploring their coping habits directly, both Lily and Daniel developed new insights about themselves and began to choose new and more healthier ways of coping. Both also recognised that a key part of coping well was having good relationships with others. The coping literature backs up their understanding of what matters most: research has found that seeking social support predicts wellbeing and longevity (Frydenberg 2022). Our role as therapists is to help our clients to think more clearly about their everyday ways of coping and to move towards more positive ways of coping by helping them to expand their vocabulary of coping. We might ask: "Do you share your problems with others?" "Do you keep your concerns to yourself?" "Do you ask for help when you need it?" Bringing the language of coping out into the open illuminates the options and helps to empower our clients.

2 Promote Empathy

> When we focus on ourselves, our world contracts as our problems and preoccupations loom large. But when we focus on others, our world expands. Our own problems drift to the periphery of the mind and so seem smaller, and we increase our capacity for connection – or compassionate action.
> Daniel Goleman, *Social Intelligence: The New Science of Human Relationships* (p. 54)
> (Goleman 2006)

Our world has become more polarised. There is greater division between political parties and less trust in institutions and the mainstream media. People are increasingly hostile towards those who are different from them. There are probably a number of reasons for this, including growing gaps in income and wealth, social media use, the decline of community institutions that once brought people together, and the loss of face-to-face interactions. Too much time spent using devices and not enough time spent experiencing genuine human connections gives rise to a specific type of person: someone who is self-centred and lacks empathy.

Therapists can do a great deal to nurture empathy and compassion for others. We child therapists can teach empathy. In his book *The War for Kindness: Building Empathy for a Fractured World* (Zaki 2019), Jamil Zaki writes that empathy is not fixed, but rather is a skill that can be developed through practice. An effective intervention is the empty chair technique made popular by Gestalt therapist Fritz Perls. I might ask my clients to imagine that a significant person is sitting in an empty chair: "What might they be thinking and feeling?" Another useful intervention is role playing. If, for example, a child seems to be struggling to understand the feelings of another person, I might invite them to role play the situation and to act out the role of the other person. This exercise helps children to get in touch with the feelings and emotions of other people.

Other useful techniques include reading storybooks—"what do you think that character is feeling?"—and loving-kindness meditations. I might say:

> Begin by taking a few slow, deep breaths. You might choose to close your eyes or look downwards. As you continue breathing slowly and deeply, I invite you to put your hands on your heart. I invite you to say silently

after me, may I be happy, may I be healthy, may I be safe, may I be calm and at ease. Imagine feelings of love and kindness shining through your whole body. I now invite you to imagine a person who loves you very much. Maybe your Mum or your Dad or a grandparent who loves you very much. Say silently after me, may that person be happy, may that person be healthy, may that person be safe, may that person be calm and at ease. Imagine feelings of love and kindness shining through and all around that person. Continue breathing slowly and deeply. I now invite you to imagine someone you don't know well. Maybe a child in another class or a neighbour you see occasionally. Say silently after me, may that person be happy, may that person be healthy, may that person be safe, may that person be calm and at ease. Imagine rays of love and kindness surrounding them. Continue breathing slowly and deeply. Now imagine someone you dislike. Maybe someone who has been rude to you. Say silently after me, may that person be happy, healthy, safe, calm and at ease. Imagine feelings of love and kindness spreading out towards them. Finally, I invite you to imagine the whole world. Say silently after me, may the whole world be happy, healthy, safe, calm and at ease. Imagine the whole world being surrounded by feelings of love and kindness.

This technique can be profoundly healing. But of course, the most powerful techniques involve focusing on present moment experiences and tuning into the feelings that are arising between us and our clients in the here-and-now. We can model empathy by striving to see things from our clients' perspectives and by reflecting back their feelings to show that we understand: "It sounds like you felt really frustrated." We can also help our clients to feel empathy towards us.

Some years ago, I treated Grace, a 10-year-old girl who was having difficulty making and keeping friends. Grace often spoke nonstop, without pausing or checking in with me, and I frequently found myself feeling distant from her. When the time felt right, I said, very gently:

"I'm curious. I've noticed that you've talked throughout our time together. And I don't think you've looked up, and I'm feeling distant from you. I feel a bit like you're talking at me and not with me. I'm wondering – is that something that happens much with your friends? How do those conversations usually go?"

For the first time, Grace lapsed into silence. Expressing my feelings prompted Grace to pause and view the situation from my perspective. It also helped her to consider the experiences of her friends.

Many of our clients have difficulties appreciating how other people are feeling, which creates challenges in their relationships. We can support them to develop healthy relationships by promoting the skill of empathy. I liken empathy to a bridge; empathy is crucial for building connections and for reducing the gap between different points of view. My middle child exudes empathy. Her warmth and ability to travel freely between viewpoints make people feel safe and inspire them to do the same, sending ripples of compassion and understanding between herself and the people around her. When we act with empathy, we benefit ourselves and others.

3 Use Fantasy

> Imagination is more important than knowledge. Knowledge is limited. Imagination encircles the world.
> Albert Einstein, *What Life Means to Einstein: An Interview by George Sylvester Viereck* (p. 117)
> (Einstein 1929)

Children often accept what they are told by adults as the objective truth even when what they are told is patently false. For example, children might be told that they're not good enough or that they are responsible for how the adults around them feel. Remember Mila, a 14-year-old child with a history of family conflict. Despite excelling academically, Mila's parents often told her that she "needed to do better at academic work." They also used shame and blame as a way to control Mila, slapping her and telling her that she was "the only child who's different" and that she "didn't care" how they felt whenever she expressed a point of view that was different from their own. When we first met, Mila believed that her experiences of being hit and criticised were to be expected and normal.

"Mila," I said. "I'm wondering about the way your parents treat you."

"Hitting is part of our culture. There's a lot of kids from our culture who get hit as a way of discipline," she remarked.

"Hmmm. I'm wondering if you could tell me more about what you think might be going on when they hit you."

"It's because I am so useless," she said sadly.

I leaned in and said gently, "I want you to know that you never deserve to be treated that way. You never deserve to be hit or put down, no matter what. You deserve to be treated with respect. You matter, and what you have to say, and your thoughts, feelings, and opinions matter."

Mila endured regular verbal attacks and believed that she was bad. My immediate task as her therapist was to help keep her safe. Later goals included helping her to see herself more accurately, helping her to recognise her core of goodness, and helping her to understand that she had a right to her own views and beliefs. I often find it useful to use fantasy to assist children like Mila to begin to express their long-hidden thoughts and ideas. Mila enjoyed writing and I invited Mila to write down what she wished for: "Mila, if you could wave a magic wand, what would your world look like? Imagine it for a little while and then write it down." Children have vivid imaginations, and fantasy provides a safe space to explore and express their wishes and to learn more about themselves and who they are. Mila wrote: "I'm in boarding school. It's easier to sleep at night. I'm with my friends all the time. I like being with my friends as much as I can. It's really good."

Many of the children I see are burdened with feelings of despair and self-doubt. As therapists, we can bring out each child's feelings and strengthen their sense of self-acceptance through fantasy. I might say: "How would you like your world to be?" "Draw your ideal world." "Draw three things that you wish for." Using fantasy sends the message to my clients that I take them and their desires seriously, and it helps them to believe in their inherent worthiness.

To illustrate: 14-year-old Malini was referred to me because she felt anxious and overwhelmed by her schoolwork. The first thing I did with Malini was to ask her to tell me what had prompted her to see me.

"I live with my parents and my eight-year-old sister. My parents are always busy. Always worrying about something or another. Half the time I'm the one looking after my sister. And my parents fight a lot. It's obvious that they don't love each other. It's never peaceful at home. Recently my grades have been dropping. I'm really worried. I don't feel like I have anyone to go to."

"It sounds like you're carrying a heavy load and it's really hard for you. And it sounds like you're feeling all alone in your worries."

"Yes. Sometimes, when I go to give my Mum a hug, she ignores me. I never get time to talk to her. My family, we never sit together. I sit on my own at the dinner table. I love my family, but my parents seem to get mad over everything. My family never have fun all together. My Dad is always on his phone. I feel like I've got my childhood taken away from me. I find it hard to catch up on school when this is happening. I'm finding it hard to focus. Worrying about stuff."

My initial priority was to be a calm presence for Malini and to provide a supportive space for her to express herself freely. In our next session, I sought to help Malini to continue to express her true feelings by inviting her to share how she would like things to be if she could wave a magic wand.

"I would want my Mum to be home more. My family would be there for me. I wouldn't have to worry about anyone or anything."

"And anything else?" I asked.

"If I had a magic wand, I would actually want me to be 18 and out of the house. Living alone. I'd have the privacy I've always wanted. I wish I had an older sibling I could relate to. I wish I could share me."

I chose this moment to ask how it felt like to relate to me.

"What is it like to share your thoughts with me?" I asked.

"I've never before gotten to open up or share before. It feels good."

Malini was extremely relieved to share many deeply personal things with me. During the next two sessions, we explored her yearnings for closeness and what typically got in the way. It became clear that to share had initially meant revealing what she perceived to be her unlikeable self. As Malini began to communicate her innermost thoughts, feelings, and hopes to me, and as I continued to offer feelings of warmth and affection, Malini's sense of self was strengthened. Through the use of fantasy and my attempts to demonstrate full acceptance of her as a person, previously unacknowledged feelings were brought out into the open, and Malini gradually began to see herself and her world more clearly, and to accept herself.

4 Help Children Identify What Is Within Their Control

...the art of being wise is the art of knowing what to overlook.
William James, *The Principles of Psychology* (p. 370)
(James 1890)

Earlier I noted that children have limited control over their lives. Children have little choice over where they live and what school they attend. They are often told what to do and how to do it. That being said, children are not entirely without control. They can make choices about how they act and respond to situations. Good child therapists help children to see what is (and what is not) within their control and to find ways to assume responsibility for the things they can control. As the Greek Stoic philosopher Epictetus observed, our primary task in life is to "identify and separate matters so that I can clearly say to myself which are externals not under my control, and which have to do with choices I actually control."

A few years ago, Noah, a 16-year-old boy reached out to me because he was feeling stressed about his upcoming end-of-year exams. We had a session with clay, and as he worked with the clay his feelings spilled out:

"I've been going back over everything and trying to learn everything, but the teachers have said you shouldn't be learning new things. There's an expectation you should know it and should be revising, not learning new things. I can't remember everything. I can't remember the terminology."

One of my first tasks was to acknowledge and reflect back Noah's feelings of worry and apprehension. Doing so gave him comfort and the strength to see his situation more clearly and to say what he really wanted:

"I'm determined to develop greater independence. I just want to finish school and be an architect. I really enjoy drawing houses. I haven't really been bothered to want the results in the past. I'm realising now it's one of the last chances to test myself. I'm more motivated to get the results. I'm more wanting to get the results."

As Noah continued to work with the clay, he continued to let go of his fears and became calmer. I then tried to help him to identify where he could step up and take more responsibility by asking: "When you think about your exams, what are the things you can control, like your own thoughts, feelings, and behaviours, and what are the things outside your control, like the weather and the behaviour of other people?" I drew two concentric circles on a piece of paper and asked him to list the things he had no control over in the outer circle, and to list the things he had direct control over in the inner circle. I find that this circle of control exercise helps children to realise that they have more control than they think and to feel empowered. I use this exercise with children aged seven and above.

Noah explained that he did not have control over how much help his teachers were willing to give him, the exam timetable, the locations of his exams, the exam seating positions, and the behaviour of the other students.

"And what do you have control over?" I asked.

"Reaching out to teachers for feedback and help. How much preparation and organisation I do. Using ChatGPT to plan the amount of time I spend on each subject. Using ChatGPT to make practice tests. How much time to spend on exam questions and knowing when to stop," he said.

I then posed two questions: "If your life was like a book, what chapter would you be in now, and what would you call it?" and "What qualities do you admire the most about yourself as you approach your exams?" I asked these questions to help Noah to realise that life didn't just happen to him: he could be the author of his life, and how he approached his life and aspects of his character were within his control.

"I usually see the good in every situation. I'm enthusiastic about certain things. I'm kind to myself and others. I'm feeling happy that I'm doing the best I can. I would be in like the third or fourth chapter of my life. This would be the largest chapter so far because there's so many new experiences and encounters. I would call it *Experiences*. From 13 to 16, you experience so much."

All children have parts of their lives that they can't control and parts that they can. Ultimately, our job is to help our clients appreciate their own role in creating the story of their lives.

5 Avoid Offering Direct Advice

I am no bird; and no net ensnares me: I am a free human being with independent will.
Charlotte Bronte, *Jane Eyre* (p. 293)
(Bronte 2006; originally published in 1847)

Adults tend to jump in and give children answers to their problems, rather than letting children work things out for themselves. Adults probably do this because they want to be helpful. They might also leap in with solutions because they find it difficult to sit with children's difficult feelings. It can be hard to witness children struggling with feelings of frustration, confusion, or distress. As child therapists, we must resist the urge to solve our clients' problems or to make decisions for them. The best child therapists help children think more clearly about their situations and make their own choices.

Long ago, a 12-year-old, Hannah, was brought in to see me by her mother because she was concerned about Hannah's anxious feelings. Hannah had been bullied the previous year at primary school: "Year 6 was a horrible year for her." According to her mother, Hannah's confidence went down, and she felt wary about being close to others. Her mother began to cry as she sat across from me: "She has shut herself off."

When I first met with Hannah on her own, I invited Hannah to do a drawing of what her anxiety looked like using lines and colours. Hannah drew a black, green, and red spiral, with heavy lines.

"Tell me about your drawing," I asked.

"It's a tunnel. It's dark," Hannah said.

"What else?" I asked.

"I always think everything is my fault. I annoy people," she said.

"Anything else?" I asked.

"The bullying was constant. Nearly every day. I still get scared that it's going to happen again. My whole body freezes. It feels really tight. It's scary. No one understands. I get upset with myself. I feel like it's always going to happen again. What should I do?" she asked.

I reflected Hannah's worries back to her, and I explained that my job was to help her to explore her challenges and to make her own decisions about what to do. I reminded Hannah that she knew herself and her situation best, and that while I could offer suggestions, only she would know what was best for her given her particular situation.

I previously described the benefits of sharing stories to instil hope. Stories and anecdotes can also be used to help our clients to explore different ways of coping with certain problems. I might say:

> Many young people your age feel anxious at times. Some feel anxious about their schoolwork, and some feel anxious about what's happening in their friendship groups. Some feel anxious about what's happening in their homes. Lots of them say that it helps just to talk to someone. They also say that it helps to practice deep breathing and to role-play certain situations. Do you think any of these things would be helpful for you?

Sometimes I find it useful to say: "Imagine that a good friend was in a similar situation to you. What would you suggest that they do?" This exercise seems to help children to think more objectively about their own situations and to come up with goals for themselves. Sometimes I simply ask: "What have you done before when you felt this way, and what helped?"

When I asked Hannah this question, she responded by saying, "I tried 4–7–8 breathing. It was good. Listening to music has helped. Writing in my journal has helped. Singing releases a lot. And I play guitar. Playing guitar has helped the most. I think that would help a lot."

Hannah initially wanted me to make decisions for her. Children need to be given the opportunity to make their own decisions and to take responsibility for their own decisions. Doing so helps them to develop confidence in their own decision-making abilities and to cultivate an understanding and acceptance of their own unique selves. I watched Hannah gain strength as she contemplated what would work best for her and made the choice to play guitar each day to ease her feelings of anxiety.

CHAPTER 7

Nurturing Growth

1 Help Children to Rediscover Their Strengths

> In each baby is a vital spark, and this urge towards life and growth is part of the baby, something the child is born with and which is carried forward in a way that we do not have to understand.
> Donald W. Winnicott, *The Child, The Family, and the Outside World* (p. 16)
> (Winnicott 2021; originally published in 1957)

Children are constantly learning new things and they can feel inadequate when they compare themselves to other children who can learn things more easily. Children are also frequently exposed to images of seemingly perfect people online, which can make them feel inferior. Most of the children I see struggle with the fear of not being good enough. They tend to focus on their weaknesses and judge themselves harshly. These feelings of insecurity seep into their relationships, including their relationship with me. They can be clingy and can continually seek my approval. In one session, Alice, a long-term client, repeatedly asked for my reassurance when I invited her to paint a picture of something that made her feel happy: "What brush should I use? How big should my painting be? Is this ok?" When I asked her to tell me something about her painting, she responded with: "Is it good?" I started to feel impatient by her neediness.

M. Andrews Luke, *A Guide to Relationship-Oriented Child Therapy*, Palgrave Texts in Counselling and Psychotherapy,
https://doi.org/10.1007/978-3-031-99658-0_7

What are my priorities in this situation? My most urgent priority was to take a moment to ground myself. My next priority was to provide a safe and supportive space so that Alice would begin to feel safe to express herself. A long-term goal was to help Alice to rediscover her strengths. The term rediscover means to find something again. Often the clients we work with are simply not aware of their own strengths. They have been buried under the weight of their negative self-perceptions. "I can't do this" was Alice's repeated refrain. She worried so much about letting others down that she did not voice her true feelings, which interfered with her ability to have deep connections with others.

Almost 10 years ago, Australian psychologist and researcher Lea Waters wrote that when parents shift their focus to their child's strengths, they can enhance their child's self-esteem and energy (Waters 2017). Therapists, too, can turn their attention to their clients' strengths. In our sixth session, I invited Alice to begin to explore her strengths using the *Strengths Cards* (2023), which are a set of illustrated cards showing animals demonstrating different strengths.

"Which of these cards are most like you?" I asked.

Alice very slowly selected three cards, "caring," "patient," and "grateful."

"It seemed hard for you to choose. What do you think about that?" I asked.

Alice bowed her head.

"What were you thinking about when you chose each card?" I asked.

"I chose caring because I'm a caring person. I care about other people," she said.

As she went on to share examples of caring for other people, she seemed to come alive, and to take great joy in recognising this part of herself.

Consider another client, Maddison, aged 11, who spoke in a very gentle voice and who seemed to depend entirely on my directives. In response to my questions, Maddison often said, "I'm not sure," and looked down. I often felt like there was a barrier between us. Using creative, strengths-based exercises allowed Maddison to identify her positive qualities and to open up. As with Alice, I invited Maddison to explore her strengths using the *Strength Cards*.

"Which are most like you?" I asked.

"Curious, practical, and generous," she said after some consideration.

"Can you draw a tree and label each branch with one of your strengths?" I asked.

As she drew, I invited her to describe a time when she had put these strengths to use.

"I have been curious and interested in a lot of different stuff. Like this morning, I saw a bug on the ground, and I was interested to know what it was. It was red and had blue wings. I'm interested in what's around me. It's hard to explain, but I know that I'm curious," she exclaimed.

"There's a real energy in you, Maddison, when you talk about your strengths. And I can't help but somehow feel closer to you."

Note that I described my observations of Maddison's behaviour, and the impact her behaviour had on me and on our relationship. As Maddison began to recognise and appreciate her unique strengths, and as she more clearly expressed her authentic self, her confidence increased, and the gap between us diminished. Four months after ending therapy, Maddison wrote me a Christmas card: *I appreciate you meeting up with me when I needed to talk to someone about how I'm feeling. I enjoyed our conversations. I felt a lot better afterwards. Thank you for helping me.* It seemed that Maddison was now able to articulate her thoughts and feelings about herself more freely.

2 Be Patient

> ...have patience with everything unresolved in your heart and try to love the questions themselves...
> Rainer Maria Rilke, *Letters to a Young Poet* (p. 14)
> (Rilke 2001; originally published in 1929)

Many well-intentioned beginning child therapists want therapy to progress quickly, and they can take it personally if their clients do not feel better straight away. This can lead to feelings of frustration and discouragement. More experienced therapists understand that therapy can take time. Building genuine therapeutic relationships with our clients happens gradually, and any positive changes in the lives of our clients tend to emerge bit-by-bit, not overnight. Being a therapist requires deep reserves of patience. We need to persevere and show up consistently for our clients, even when our work together seems slow.

Earlier I described Sienna, a 10-year-old client who often refused to engage in the work of therapy. She rarely spoke and was wary about trying new things, both in the therapy room and in her daily life. Despite my best efforts to meet her where she was at, and to go at her pace, I sometimes found myself hurrying her along, which didn't help. Trying to rush her only shut her down more. On these occasions, our interactions were very one-sided, and I was often left feeling depleted.

How to shift from impatience to patience? The word "patience" comes from the Latin word "patientia," which means a willingness to endure adversities and suffering calmly. In future sessions, I tried to approach Sienna's struggles to express herself with more compassion, and to accept her where she was. To illustrate: one day Sienna's mother told me that Sienna had a school camp coming up and that she was refusing to attend. I began the next session with Sienna by referring back to our previous session, knowing that Sienna would bring the issue of going to camp out into the open if it was important to her.

"The last time we met, you worked with some clay. I wonder how you felt afterwards?" I asked.

Sienna looked up at me and said, "My mum said I have to go to camp next week. I hate all camps. I don't think I'll do all the activities. I'll refuse to do the climbing activities. I know I'm not going to do the climbing activities."

In that moment, as feelings of irritation once again started to rise in me, I reminded myself to be patient. I tried to be empathetic and to remember that Sienna had learned at some point to be uncooperative in order to protect herself against the possibility of negative judgements from others.

"I know that going on camp is hard for you," I said gently.

"I can do the climbing activities. I just don't want to do them," she said.

"You just don't want to do those activities," I reflected back, softly.

After offering Sienna my empathy and calmly accepting her reluctance, I noticed a small shift in Sienna. Her stance began to soften.

"I just don't know if I can do them. I don't know what the activities are," she said slowly.

"You're not sure if you can do them, and you don't actually know what might be involved. What might happen if you did give them a try?" I asked.

"I don't know," she said quietly.

After a period of silence, I chose to shift the topic to tennis, which was her passion:

"Sienna, you say that you're not sure if you'll be able to do the climbing activities. You've also told me how much you love playing tennis, and how hard you try when you're playing tennis. The climbing activities might be like stepping up to serve for the first time in a big match. You're not sure where exactly the ball will land, but you won't know until you take the shot. Even if you miss, you can try again. I wonder if it would help to think about the climbing activities in the same way."

Sienna let her guard down and said, "I sometimes get my first serve in. If I don't get it in, I hit it a bit softer. I guess I could give the climbing activities a try."

What a joy it was to watch Sienna have the courage to share her difficult feelings and to then open up to the possibility of trying a new thing. Of course, it wasn't so much the tennis metaphor or my suggestion that helped, but the care and kindness I had shown her. We must remind ourselves that therapy cannot be hurried, and that it is ultimately the quality of the therapeutic relationship that facilitates the process of change. Just we cannot force a river to flow more rapidly, we cannot force our clients to change quickly through our sheer will. Do you have the patience to gently tend to your relationships with your clients and wait for the work of therapy to flow at its own pace?

3 Repair Any Ruptures

> …no matter how skilled we are, we will occasionally drift away from present awareness. If a client notices this and brings it to our attention, we can shift our focus back to the client and repair this lapse.
> Gerald Corey, *Personal Reflections on Counseling* (p. 151)
> (Corey 2020)

Therapy is a relationship. As with any working relationship between people, there are missteps, mistakes, and misunderstandings. I've had many lapses, especially when I was starting out as a therapist. Children are often very aware of their exact age, and they love sharing the precise details about their age because their age is a source of pride: "I'm five and a half." A long time ago, I saw a client and forgot her age. "You must be about nine," I stumbled. She was actually 10, and my words stunned her. "I'm 10!" she exclaimed, alarmed that I didn't get it right.

Therapy is about being in the here-and-now, but I sometimes find myself feeling bored and losing concentration. I've stifled yawns. I've also had moments when I've been unable to remember important names. I have occasionally made assumptions about my clients' interests and abilities without checking first. Sometimes I just do not listen well, particularly when I am feeling under pressure.

Even the most experienced therapists slip up. It is our job to apologise for our mistakes and to repair any ruptures. We might say simply: "I'm sorry." All of the children I've apologised to over the years have been grateful for my words of remorse. Unfortunately, adults can find it hard to say sorry to children. There could be several reasons. Difficulty expressing emotions. A fragile sense of self. A need for control. Such adults do not seem to understand that offering children a genuine apology actually builds respect. When we offer our clients a genuine apology, we not only build respect: we also send our clients the message that we care about them and about our relationships with them, which strengthens our relationships with them.

We must also learn from our lapses and avoid repeating them. To avert dips in focus, we might practice mindfulness before we meet with our clients. To prevent slips of memory, we might read over our clients' notes carefully. It is also good practice to make a point of asking our clients to share their perspectives on how we could do better next time. Think of what I said earlier about using Scott Miller's *Child Session Rating Scale* to obtain feedback at the end of each session (Duncan, Miller et al. 2003). I gain a lot of useful information using this scale.

Donald W. Winnicott writes of the "good enough" parent as someone who is tuned into their child's needs and who responds sensitively, but who is not perfect, and notes that this imperfection ultimately helps their child to be resilient and cope well in an imperfect world (Winnicott 2021; originally published in 1957). Just as children benefit from imperfect parents, they also benefit from imperfect therapists. Children need to learn that relationships are messy at times because they involve people with different needs, preferences, and ways of seeing. By modelling how to repair any ruptures in our therapeutic relationships with our clients, we teach our clients about what good relationships look like, and we teach them that it's ok not to be perfect. We are all human. We all make mistakes. What matters is what we do with those mistakes.

4 Give Good Compliments

I can live for two months on a good compliment.
Mark Twain

When I started studying psychology in the 1990s, the self-esteem movement was in full swing. The movement was based on the idea that low self-esteem leads to problems such as drug abuse, unemployment, and crime, and that high self-esteem is necessary for success in life. Everyone was determined to make children feel good by praising them all the time: "You're the best," "You're brilliant," "You're so smart," "You can do anything."

The problem with this type of all-encompassing praise is that it sends children the message that they don't have to work on their abilities. In her book, *Mindset*, American psychologist and researcher Carol Dweck suggests that children who receive inflated praise can come to believe that their abilities are fixed, which then makes them afraid of challenges and sensitive to criticism (Dweck 2012; originally published in 2006). In short, over-praising damages self-esteem and makes children worry about meeting such high standards. On the other hand, children who understand that their abilities can be cultivated through hard work are willing to take on challenges and are motivated to see them through. They have what Dweck refers to as a growth mindset.

How to help enhance our clients' feelings about themselves without resorting to blanket praise? When I see a child in therapy, I do all of the things I've described so far. I show them respect. I take them seriously. I tell them the truth. I listen to them deeply. I invite them to share their innermost feelings. I also give them compliments, but I take care to make them specific. To my mind, the best compliments are those that are sharp, sincere, and spoken from the heart.

For example, a 16-year-old girl I was seeing talked about how hard she was finding the last week of the school year:

"I've got no motivation to do anything. I'm just so tired. I want the holidays to come. My friends are changing up and it's so annoying. They're so annoying. One of my friends deliberately tripped me up the other day. They all thought it was funny. They are so obnoxious. They just need to grow up a bit. I started vaping again. Twice."

After acknowledging her feelings of despair and disappointment, I made the following comment:

"You know, we've been meeting for a couple of months now, and we've talked a lot about your frustration about the behaviour of your friends, and how hard it has been for you to stop vaping."

"Yeah, I started again. I'm hopeless," she interrupted.

"I was thinking the opposite. I can see that it's been really hard for you to stop. And I want you to know that I really admire your dedication to stop, and your commitment to trying new things. You've been using nicotine patches and gum. You've been doing breathing exercises. I also admire your willingness to share just how hard it's been with me, and your honesty about your setbacks. You say that you've got no motivation to do anything, but there's a part of you that's so motivated that you are here today. I admire your motivation to come here each week and face your challenges, head-on."

Note my liberal use of "I-statements." The effort she had put in was huge, and by sharing my own positive sentiments about her hard work and courage, I hoped to convey to her my deep respect, support, and wholehearted acceptance of her, flaws and all. Give your clients compliments, but be sure to make them precise and personal. Your openness and authenticity will soothe your clients and will encourage your clients to relate more openly with you.

5 Recognise When It's Time to End Therapy

> Every new beginning comes from some other beginning's end.
> Seneca

The question of when to end therapy can be a difficult one. There is no simple answer. It depends on the complexities of the child's needs and their situation. It can take a while for children to open up, tell their stories, and work through their strong emotions. Parents sometimes want a quick fix for their child, but some problems can't be fixed quickly. Recall my earlier comments about the importance of being patient. Most children, however, do not need long-term, ongoing therapy. They don't carry around as much emotional baggage as adults. I usually meet with children for 5 to 20 sessions. Occasionally a single session is enough. A meta-analytic review of child-centred play therapy found that the average number of sessions was 11.87 (Lin and Bratton 2015).

It's important to be continuously looking out for the signs that our clients might be ready to end therapy: Has the child stopped having strong emotional responses in therapy? For example, do they seem less fearful? Less angry? Less lonely? Do they seem calmer and more content? Do they say that they are doing well on the *Child Outcome Rating Scale* (Miller and Duncan 2000)? Is the child "playing" in therapy rather than engaging in deep therapeutic work? Has the child reached a plateau? Have their behaviours improved? Is the child indicating that they want a break from sessions? Are the parents hinting that they might want to discontinue sessions? These are all clues that it might be time to end treatment.

I make sure to give children plenty of warning about the end of therapy. First, I introduce the idea gently. I then take care to ask each child how they might feel about therapy ending. I might say the following: "Things seem to be going well. You've let me know that you're doing well. It might be a good time to start thinking about stopping our time together. I wonder how you feel about that?" Sometimes children struggle with the end of therapy. Sometimes their behaviour takes a step backwards. I might decide that they aren't ready to stop just yet. If I judge that it is time to stop, I might meet them two or three times over the next month. In my view, one session is usually not enough time to end the therapeutic relationship. Don't rush the final sessions.

A colleague once told me that she invited children to decorate and fill a small cardboard box with meaningful things at the end of therapy. I like this closing technique. It can be difficult to let go of the therapeutic relationship. Objects can help ease the transition. Most children have been on holiday with a suitcase, so I invite them to imagine that the cardboard box is a suitcase and to decorate it. I find that most children are eager to do this activity. I might say:

> Let's close our eyes and take a few deep breaths. I invite you to think about our time together, what we have done together, and what we have talked about. Let's think about that for a little while...I now invite you to open your eyes and to decorate this cardboard box with things that remind you of the things that have happened. I invite you to imagine that this box is a suitcase. You can take it with you at the end of our time together. You may choose how to decorate your suitcase. Some children like to use

> different colours or words or pictures. It's up to you. I also invite you to fill your suitcase with whatever you want. You can cut out pictures from these magazines or you might like to draw your own pictures or write your own messages. Some children write messages about what we have talked about.

My intention, of course, is to help children "take home" what they have learned about themselves. I never know where this activity will take us. One nine-year-old girl, Evelyn, wrote the following messages on pieces of coloured paper: "Take deep breaths," "Pat Charlie [her dog]," "Think of your calm spot." These were her new ways of coping. If I have scanned children's previous drawings, I pull them up on my laptop and we look at them together. In our final conversations, I always make a point of letting each child know that I liked meeting with them, that I care about them, that I will miss seeing them, and that I believe they are ready for the next part of their journey. I also mention that they can see me again if they think it would be helpful. I might say that it's normal to feel sad when we stop meeting with someone we care about. Saying goodbye is hard. Children often write notes of farewell to me. One child wrote: *Thank you so much for everything you've done and helped me through. I'm forever grateful for everything you've done for me*. You will come up with your own creative and gentle ways of closing therapy with your clients.

PART III

The Family

CHAPTER 8

Including Families in the Therapeutic Process

1 Expand Your Focus to Include Each Child's Family

> It can be tempting to believe that each of us has more control over our own fate than we actually do. The truth is that we are all embedded in ecologies bigger than ourselves that shape us in profound ways. Economies, cultures, and subcultures all play important roles in what we believe, how we behave, and the progression of our lives. None of these ecologies is more important than that of the family.
> Robert Waldinger and Marc Schulz, *The Good Life* (p. 201)
> (Waldinger and Schulz 2023)

Many therapists tend to focus on individual clients and individual mental health and overlook their clients' significant relationships. It is possible that therapists prioritise individual therapy because their training programs emphasised individual therapy models. It might also be due to convenience. Involving multiple people can be challenging. But we are profoundly influenced by the relationships we have with the people around us. Our relationships are often the primary source of our suffering and our healing. We child therapists need to connect our clients' challenges and positive growth to the people who populate their lives, including their family members.

M. Andrews Luke, *A Guide to Relationship-Oriented Child Therapy*, Palgrave Texts in Counselling and Psychotherapy,
https://doi.org/10.1007/978-3-031-99658-0_8

The Russian-born American developmental psychologist Uri Bronfenbrenner spoke of the impact of relationships on child development:

> In order to develop – intellectually, emotionally, socially, and morally – a child requires participation in progressively more complex reciprocal activity, on a regular basis over an extended period in the child's life, with one or more persons with whom the child develops a strong, mutual, irrational, emotional attachment. (Bronfenbrenner 1991, p. 2)

A key example of a long-lasting attachment is the parent–child relationship, which often lays the foundation for the child's future growth and development. Positive child development requires responsive parents or caregivers. In a meta-analytic review of play therapy treatment outcomes, Sue C. Bratton and her colleagues found that involving parents enhances therapeutic success (Bratton, Ray et al. 2005). It goes without saying that the best child therapists seek to actively involve parents in their work with children and to support caring family relationships.

I usually speak on the phone to the parents before meeting with the child. During this phone call, I outline the therapy process and other practical considerations, such as how to get to my office. Parents often start to describe their child's difficulties during this phone call. I explain that I would prefer to wait until we meet in person, when there will be more time. I try to meet with the parents and the child in the first session. I occasionally invite siblings to attend. At this first session, I invite the family to share what prompted them to reach out to me. I find it helpful to ask: "Why now?" The parents will often speak first. I make a point of asking about the child's point of view: "Is that how you see things?"

I do my best to maintain an attitude of warm, open curiosity towards the parents. I take great care to listen well and show respect. I might offer the parents a glass of water or a cup of tea or coffee. Parents can be anxious, and I strive to show them compassion. Having said this, nothing is more important than my relationship with the child. At all times, I make an effort to demonstrate genuine interest and non-judgemental acceptance towards the child. If the parents try to dominate the conversation, I put a stop to it. I regularly ask the child: "What do you think?"

In this initial session with the family, I go over what therapy is and the ground rules, including confidentiality. I always make a point of emphasising that I will check with the child before sharing any information with the parents or any other people. I mention that I will probably meet face-to-face with the family together again, but that I will talk about this possibility with the child first. By including the child fully in the initial session, I hope to convey to the child from the outset that they are seen and heard and that they matter to me. Children can feel invisible. I feel certain that these acts of empathy and respect do a lot to build trust in the beginning stages of my relationship with the child.

When I first meet with children alone, I often invite them to do a drawing of their family and to describe their family as they draw.

For example, I asked a seven-year-old girl, Aria, to do a drawing of her family and to describe what she likes doing with each family member:

"I like playing Uno with my Dad. I like making pizza with my Mum. I like going to dog shows with my family. I like playing with our dogs with my sister. I really like going outside on the trampoline with my brother. I like doing outside things with my brother."

I learn a lot about each child's family relationships from these drawings. As the child talks, I listen not just to their words but to their tone of voice. I carefully watch their facial expressions and how they draw each family member. I am interested in their feelings about their family members. This particular type of drawing activity can be a gentle window into their perceptions about what is going on in their families. With the child's permission, I describe their drawings and share other important information about our sessions with their parents. In general, both children and parents welcome and value the sharing of information. These conversations with parents are a critical part of the therapeutic process for me.

For too long, our focus has been too narrow. Children need families, and we therapists need to expand our focus and enthusiastically include parents and families in the therapeutic process. In short, I suggest involving parents as much as possible. You will develop your own ways of involving parents.

2 Understand How Family Systems Work

> No one person can see the whole picture because he is limited to his own perspective. By having everyone together we can get the whole picture more clearly. Every person has a unique contribution to make which cannot be duplicated by anyone else.
> Virginia Satir, *Conjoint Family Therapy* (p. 141)
> (Satir 1983; originally published in 1964)

When parents walk into the first meeting, they often begin by implying that the child is the one with the problem and they are focused on changing the child. But in the practice of child therapy, it is evident that the child's behaviour is profoundly influenced by their family relationships. This is common sense. Children spend most of their time with their families. Their struggles are inextricably linked to their family relationships. Context matters.

I believe that family systems theory is a good frame of reference for understanding and helping children. Family systems theory has its origins in both general systems theory and the theory of cybernetics. The term "general systems theory" was first used in the 1940s by Ludwig von Bertalanffy, an Austrian biologist (von Bertalanffy 1950). He viewed organisms as complex systems with interdependent parts: changing one part of a system may affect the other parts of the system. At around the same time, the term "cybernetics" was coined by Norbert Wiener, an American mathematician and philosopher (Wiener 1948). He realised that almost all systems, such as biological systems and computing systems, process information and regulate themselves through circular feedback loops. Communication does not just flow one way; it is an interactive process.

Before general systems and cybernetics theory, therapists often believed that a person's struggles could be traced back to a specific cause. From the 1950s onwards, therapists started to draw on the idea that a person's challenges could be influenced by multiple, interacting factors, including family dynamics. In 1955, American psychiatrist and family therapist Murray Bowen began working on his concept of "triangles," which describes the way that two people tend to "triangle in" a third person to help regulate or relieve any anxiety between the original two people (Goding 1992). In troubled families, one family member might pull in another family member when they are having a disagreement with a third family member.

During the 1960s and early-to-mid-1970s, Argentine-American family therapist Salvador Minuchin came up with the concepts of "subsystems" and "boundaries" (Minuchin 1974). Subsystems include individuals, the spouse or partner subsystem, the parental subsystem, the sibling subsystem, and intergenerational subsystems. Boundaries are the generally invisible rules that control how, when, and to what degree subsystems relate to each other. In his final book, *The Craft of Family Therapy* (Minuchin, Reiter and Borda 2021), Minuchin states that: "Families have a variety of subsystems, though they often do not understand the reality and complexity of how they function. When therapists highlight these aspects, members can be moved beyond the rigid patterns they have been repeating" (p. 8).

American social worker Virgina Satir expressed a similar view. While working at the Illinois State Psychiatric Institute in the 1950s, she began developing her approach to family therapy, which emphasised the importance of drawing attention to the "communication patterns" between family members and the overt and covert rules that govern how families operate (Satir 1983; originally published in 1964). In her book, *Conjoint Family Therapy* (Satir 1983; originally published in 1964), Satir writes that: "Closed systems are those in which every participating member must be very cautious about what he says. The principal rule seems to be that everyone is supposed to have the same opinions, feelings, and desires, whether or not this is true" (p. 237). Satir's systems-oriented approach is consistent with my experience working with families. I find that healthy families have direct and clear patterns of communication and flexible rules. Family members say what they mean and mean what they say, and there is room for disagreement.

In her book, *Your Family Revealed*, psychotherapist Elaine Carney Gibson suggests asking the following questions to help bring family dynamics to the surface: How does the family system operate? How does it affect the child? What are the unspoken rules? Are the triangles healthy or unhealthy? Do the family relationships allow the child to be an individual and to grow and thrive? Is the child free to have their own thoughts and feelings? Are they free to express themselves? Are their needs listened to or are they dismissed (Gibson 2023)? Gibson also draws on the narrative approach developed by family therapists Michael White and David Epston (White and Epston 1990) and suggests paying attention to the stories people tell themselves about their families and the meanings they give to those stories: what are the family's stories? How have they shaped the way that people see themselves and relate to each other?

In my meetings with families, I might ask: "How do you share what you're thinking and feeling with each other?" "How does your family handle disagreements?" "Can you tell me about a time when you felt really connected as a family, and why?" "Can you take turns saying something that you like about each other?" I might ask individual family members: "What's it like for you to be in your family?" "How do you think your behaviour might be affecting the rest of your family?" "Are there any changes you would like to see in your family relationships?" I might ask the child: "Can you help me to understand what your parents are saying?" I often make an effort to seek greater clarification: "Can you tell me more?" "Can you give me an example?" "Could you be more concrete?" My aims are twofold: first, I want to help improve communication between family members, and second, I want to promote greater connection.

Families don't often have these types of conversations. When my oldest daughter was 13, we attended a parent–child workshop led by an organisation called Time & Space. In small groups, the parents were invited to share the joys and challenges of being the parent of a teenager, and the teenagers were invited to share the joys and challenges of being a teenager. We also shared one thing we admired about our respective child or parent. There was lots of laughter. Tears flowed freely. Many children (and parents) say that they do not feel heard. These types of opportunities help everyone to express their feelings and feel heard, seen, understood, and valued. Systems thinking allows us child therapists to look beyond the narrow view and to strengthen the child's relationships with their family. I encourage you to widen your lens and see the bigger picture.

3 Observe Family Dynamics

> Happy families are all alike; every unhappy family is unhappy in its own way.
> Leo Tolstoy, *Anna Karenina* (p. 3)
> (Tolstoy 1992; originally published in 1878)

I believe that one of our main tasks in child therapy is to keep a close eye on family interactions. How does the child relate to the parents? How do the parents relate to the child? Are they warm or polite or distant? How does everyone express their thoughts and feelings? Directly or indirectly or in a passive-aggressive way? Do they use words? Do they use a particular tone of voice? Are they open or cautious? Leaning back or hunched over? Do they make eye contact or look away? Do they listen to each other? Do they nod or frown? Is there a lot of affirmation or criticism? Are they physically affectionate or at arm's length from each other? What feelings are being conveyed? My job is to detect patterns of communication between the child and the parents.

A decade ago, I saw a 17-year-old girl, Lily. She was described by one of her teachers as: "Withdrawn and disengaged. She's struggling to concentrate." In the initial family meeting, I invited Lily and her mother to describe why they had come in: "As you were walking to my office, were you thinking about anything in particular that you wanted to cover today?" Lily's mother led the conversation: "Lily lacks discipline. She doesn't work hard enough. If she put in more effort, she would be doing much better." I could sense her fury. Her brows were furrowed, and her lips were pressed together in a tight line. I could also see Lily withdrawing. Her arms were crossed, and she had a blank face. With each of her mother's words, Lily sank more deeply into her chair. Lily's mother looked off into the distance. She was not tuned into Lily or her needs. Her attitude of anger and disappointment seemed to be a major source of Lily's problems. I asked Lily's mother to direct her words to Lily using "I feel" statements:

"Sometimes it can be helpful to express ourselves using sentences that start with the words, 'I feel.' You might have heard of this before. Can you please direct your words to Lily starting with the words, 'I feel'?"

"I feel mad when you don't do your work," she said.

"Please say more about this to Lily," I said.

"Lily, I want you to have a better job than I have. I am worried about your future. I want you to succeed in life," she pleaded.

"Lily, what is it like to hear your Mum say that? Can you please direct your words to your Mum?" I asked.

"I understand that you want what's best for me, but you're so focused on me studying pharmacy. You're obsessed with the idea. I want to make you happy, but I just don't want to be a pharmacist," she said.

"I didn't know that," her mother responded quietly. She softened as she started to see Lily's true feelings for the first time.

Naturally, my intention here was to help Lily and her mother relate more directly to each other. My observations guided me. They provided me with rich information about what was happening and why and how to direct the conversation. People often talk about generation gaps. Generation gaps do not have to be relational gaps. I'm always on the look out for relational gaps between children and their parents. By helping children and their families to give expression to their feelings, we help to close relational gaps.

4 Teach Parents About Normal Child Development and Behaviour

It is a wise father that knows his own child.
William Shakespeare, *The Merchant of Venice* (p. 60)
(Shakespeare 1600)

So far, we have considered the importance of involving parents in the work of child therapy and the benefits of using family systems thinking to explore the influence of family interactions on children. We have also considered how we might help parents and children to relate to each other more openly by encouraging them to communicate with each other directly during the therapeutic hour. I believe that supporting families to communicate clearly in the present moment is one of the best ways to work with families because it is immediate and impactful.

Despite the advantages of working in the here-and-now, parents frequently cry out for specific instructions and guidelines about their children. How to respond? I do not tell parents directly what to do, but I am prepared to teach parents about normal child development and behaviour. Families have changed enormously over the last century. Family members tend to live further apart, households are smaller, and parents don't often have day-to-day support and guidance from caring grandparents, aunts, and uncles. Giving parents information about the behaviours of children helps parents to have realistic expectations of their children and can help to reduce any anxiety, frustration, and stress that they may feel. It can also help parents to view their child's behaviour through a more compassionate lens.

If parents want to know if it's normal for their child to be behaving in a particular way, I try to answer them directly. If it feels right, I will often pre-empt questions from parents by sharing things like the following: it's normal for pre-school aged children to have meltdowns and to experience difficulties sharing. They are still learning how to manage their big feelings. It's not unusual for children aged five to nine to regress when they have experienced big changes or are feeling stressed. For example, they might revert back to feeling anxious about being separated from their parents, or they might wet the bed. It's normal for children aged 10–12 to feel self-conscious about how they are perceived by others and for their interests to change as they start to explore who they are. It's very common for teenagers to have fluctuating moods, to want privacy, and to question the rules. They are developing their own identity.

I will often say to parents that it can also be useful to consider the duration, intensity, and impact of their child's behaviour. Has the behaviour persisted over an extended time? How intense is the behaviour? Is the behaviour interfering with the child's everyday life? If the behaviour has lasted for weeks and is causing distress, I will usually say that therapy is advisable.

I always add that the child is doing what they are doing to cope with their situation and to meet their own needs, even if their behaviours do not make logical sense. They might be behaving aggressively because they feel powerless, and aggression gives them a sense of control. They might be withdrawing because they have been bullied, and they are avoiding getting hurt again. They might be injuring themselves to release emotional pain. They might be starving themselves because it gives them a sense of mastery. Of utmost importance, however, is listening to and acknowledging everyone's feelings about the behaviours. It is essential that these feelings are thoroughly explored and are given an opportunity to come out. As the family members share their feelings, I invariably observe a softening taking place.

Effective child therapy often involves teaching parents about normal child development and how they might make sense of their child's behaviours so that the parents can better understand and have greater empathy for their child. Accepting children for who they are helps children to accept themselves. Ultimately, these types of explanations help to promote understanding and compassion rather than judgement and blame and strengthen the parent–child relationship.

5 Teach Relationship Skills

> Evidence is accumulating that human beings of all ages are happiest and able to deploy their talents to best advantage when they are confident that, standing behind them, there are one or more trusted persons who will come to their aid should difficulties arise. The person trusted, also known as an attachment figure (Bowlby 1969), can be considered as providing his (or her) companion with a secure base from which to operate.
> John Bowlby, *The Making and Breaking of Affectional Bonds* (pp. 124–125).
> (Bowlby 2005; originally published in 1979)

> There is something simple and life affirming in the attachment message that the only thing your child needs in order to thrive emotionally is your emotional availability and responsiveness.
> Robert Karen, *Becoming Attached* (p. 17).
> (Karen 1990, February)

What do parents want for their children? When I ask parents what they want for their child during our first meeting, they usually say that they just want their child to be happy. Unfortunately, this can sometimes result in parents jumping in and attempting to solve their children's problems for them. But when parents try to take over whenever their children feel upset, this only hinders their children's capacity to cope with uncomfortable feelings and the inevitable challenges of life. Many parents also find themselves buying their children material possessions like toys, gadgets, and clothes in the hope that this too will make their children happy. Parents, like all of us, can sometimes lose sight of the fact that close and supportive relationships, and respectfully allowing children to face their own challenges, are key to children's wellbeing and happiness.

Long ago, John Bowlby, a psychiatrist and one of the founders of attachment theory, pointed out that when parents offer their children strong and consistent caregiving and support their children to "deal with the world" their children are more likely to be self-reliant (Bowlby 2005; originally published in 1979; p. 130). Mary Ainsworth, a developmental psychologist and co-founder of attachment theory, worked closely with Bowlby at the Tavistock Clinic in London between 1950 and 1954 and expanded on his work. In the 1960s, she developed the "Strange Situation Procedure" and came up with the concept of a "secure base" (Ainsworth and Bell 1970). She believed that children used one or more "attachment figures" as a base from which to explore their world, and she argued that children displayed three broad patterns of exploratory behaviour: anxious-ambivalent (also called anxious-resistant), anxious-avoidant, and secure.

Ainsworth posited that children who use an anxious-ambivalent strategy have not experienced consistent parental availability. They may be clingy and highly distressed when their parents leave them, and they can be in two minds—needy and angry—when their parents return. They are hard to comfort, and they have difficulty with intimate relationships. Children who use an anxious-avoidant strategy have parents who are consistently emotionally unresponsive or dismissive, and they explore their environment with apparent independence. These children appear indifferent to their parents and avoid seeking comfort from their parents when they are distressed. They learn to feel uncomfortable relying on others. In contrast, children who are secure have parents who are both emotionally attuned and consistent in their responses. These children actively explore their environment, and they can depend on their parents. When they get upset, they seek comfort from their parents, and they are easily soothed. They usually have trusting relationships with others. In the classic book, *Patterns of Attachment*, Ainsworth and her colleagues write that, "few if any adults cease to be influenced by their early attachments" (Ainsworth, Blehar et al. 2015; originally published in 1978; p. 21).

The simple message of both Bowlby's and Ainsworth's work is that the quality of the parent–child relationship paves the way for the child's well-being and relationships later in life. Both Bowlby and Ainsworth implored clinicians to embrace their ideas. Most child therapists are told to read their texts during their training. But how exactly can child therapists help parents to be a secure base for their child and to strengthen the parent–child bond?

I've already spoken about teaching parents the skills of clear communication. Child therapists can also teach the skills of reflective listening. I tell parents that reflective listening is a way of listening that involves mirroring back both the content of what was said and the feelings expressed. I give examples to help illustrate what reflective listening looks like: "It sounds like you're worried about the test tomorrow." "You're feeling happy with the picture you drew." "Not making the team is really frustrating." "It looks like you're excited about going on school camp but also a bit nervous."

I explain that reflective listening begins with tuning in to the child's specific feelings. I say that it is about paying close attention to the child, showing the child that they are genuinely interested in their world and who they are, and really listening to them. I remind parents again and again that it is not about agreeing with the child or offering them advice or solutions. Rather, it is about being a soothing presence for the child.

Reflective listening helps parents to truly relate to their children and to see their children as unique and separate individuals with their own needs, feelings, and hopes. It helps children to feel understood, loved, and valued, and to open up and say what they really want, feel, and believe. Children flourish when they feel heard and accepted by their parents: "My parents get it. They know who I am. They are here to help me when I need it, and I can rely on them. I can trust them." "I am my own self, but I am not alone. I am loved." "I feel good about who I am. I am confident. I can trust myself."

CHAPTER 9

Strengthening Families

1 Affirm Families

> Families for all their flaws are one of our remaining ancient and true shelters. Families, not therapists, will be there for our clients if they lose their jobs, go to hospital, or need someone to show up at their bowling tournaments.
> Mary Pipher, *Letters to a Young Therapist* (p. 31)
> (Pipher 2016; originally published in 2003)

> You are all family to me.
> Murrundindi

One of my most treasured relationships is with Murrundindi. He is the Ngurungaeta (Head Man) and Elder of the Wurundjeri tribe, the traditional custodians of the land in and around Melbourne, Australia. A calm, dignified man, Murrundindi has kind eyes and a gentle smile that puts everyone at ease. He is a great leader and teacher, and he has shared his culture in schools and at the Healesville Sanctuary for more than four decades. I met Murrundindi in 2021, and he has given me many gifts. During the past few years, I have spent about one day a month with him. We sit outside with groups of children near some red river gums in Berwick, and he tells stories. His storytelling consists of many components: humour, singing, music, and dance, and he models integrity and

M. Andrews Luke, *A Guide to Relationship-Oriented Child Therapy*, Palgrave Texts in Counselling and Psychotherapy,
https://doi.org/10.1007/978-3-031-99658-0_9

love. Murrundindi's stories bring children together. The way I see it, Murrundindi is the best storyteller.

After each morning of storytelling, we have an hour-long, two-course lunch together, and we talk about Aboriginal and Torres Strait Islander ways of understanding psychology and traditional healing practices. Our conversations range from yidaki (didgeridoo) healing to smoking ceremonies to welcoming children and giving them a manna gum leaf ("a passport onto our Country") to learning from Elders. After lunch, we return to the river red gums. I love my time with Murrundindi, and he has served as a great mentor to me. His teachings have changed my life. I have learned so much from Murrundindi about our need for meaningful human connections. Murrundindi often says to children, in his gentle and reassuring voice:

"I call everyone Kirrip. Kirrip means family. We are all one big family. You are my family. You are like my grandchildren. I respect you like my grandchildren. If you ever need my help, you ask me. I'll be there for you. To support you. I'll support you in any sort of way I can. Because that's what I've been put here to do. To help people. You are safe with me."

As I write, I see children looking up at him and into his eyes.

In Aboriginal cultures, everyone is kin. All people—and all ancestral beings, plants, animals, land, and sea—are linked through a kinship network, and wellbeing is deeply influenced by relationships, including relationships with blood and non-blood relations or kin. Murrundindi understands that. We all turn to our biological or chosen family members for help and comfort in times of need. I once asked Murrundindi why families are so essential. He replied immediately:

"It all starts with the family and the community. By all coming together and working together. We've all got to come together in harmony and peace and respect one another. And if you've got a strong community, and you teach your children about respect for the land and respect for one another, and that comes from the whole community, then that will be passed down through generations. It's all about community and all about working together as one."

In Western societies, the emphasis on individualism can sometimes result in more time spent focusing on individual achievement and less time spent nurturing family bonds. But when family relationships are strong and healthy, children are strong and healthy. In their book *The Good Life: Lessons from the World's Longest Scientific Study of Happiness*,

Robert Waldinger and Marc Schulz write that "enriching these relationships despite challenges, persevering, and appreciating the positive things we get from them is worth the trouble" (Waldinger and Schulz 2023, p. 219). Child therapists can acknowledge, support, encourage, affirm, and validate families. We can help families to understand their worth. I take care to ask the families I work with questions like: "Can you tell me a time when you overcame a challenge together?" "What's something you're proud of as a family?" "What are some of your family's greatest strengths?" My aim, of course, is to highlight the vital importance of families and to help families to have confidence in themselves.

"Murrundindi" means home in the mountain. Just as Murrundindi's presence is like a soothing shelter, so too is the presence of our family members. Children can only flourish when they are connected to something bigger than themselves, such as their families. Our job is to support and prioritise the value of families. To quote Spanish-American philosopher George Santayana: "The family is one of nature's masterpieces."

2 Affirm Parents

> The role of the therapist in the interview with the parents was to convey a belief that they were the best authorities in deciding how they should act in the relations with their child.
> Clark E. Moustakas, *Children in Play Therapy* (p. 104)
> (Moustakas 1953)

A few other suggestions about giving information or advice to parents. Offer guidance to parents tentatively. It is counterproductive to tell parents exactly what to do. Do not put pressure on parents to act in a particular way. I make a point of saying to parents: "You know your child and your family best. How does what I've shared with you fit with what you know about your child and your family?" I accept whatever they conclude.

In Part II, I write about relating to children with warmth and respect. I approach parents in the same way. Parents are often upset and bewildered by their children's feelings of distress. In my view, communicating my care and my belief in their ability to make the best decisions about their child increases their trust in me and their confidence in their parenting abilities.

In the 1950s, Clark E. Moustakas, a founding member of the humanistic psychology movement who studied with Virginia Axline, started seeing children and their parents at the Merrill-Palmer Institute in Detroit. He recorded every session to try to pinpoint the key therapeutic factors in child therapy (Blau 2013). In his first book, *Children in Play Therapy*, he emphasised the vital significance of the therapeutic relationship (Moustakas 1953). He also emphasised the importance of being an empathetic listener with parents and of encouraging parents to trust their inner resources. Likewise, Donald W. Winnicott said that, "It is when a mother trusts her own judgement that she is at her best" (Winnicott 2021; originally published in 1957; p. 13).

I have found that there is a tendency among some professionals to find fault with parents. Our job as child therapists is to support and empower parents rather than to criticise them. Murrundindi often speaks of holding parents and grandparents in the highest regard. In Murrundindi's terms:

"You have to respect your Elders because they're your leaders, they're your teachers, they give you the knowledge that has been passed down to them. And by showing respect, you get more knowledge. I always respected my Elders. I respected my grandmother and my grandfather, and I respected my parents. It's about respect. Showing respect to one another. You've got to look up to your Elders. By looking up to your Elders that's showing respect to one another."

Child therapists must take care to openly appreciate the knowledge, experience, and insights of parents.

Acknowledging the demands of being a parent is also essential. In an initial conversation with parents, I might say, for example:

> Being a parent is hard work. It's often described as the hardest job in the world. I sometimes say to parents that it can be easier to look after other children than it is to look after our own children. I also know firsthand how challenging it can be to juggle the demands of family and work and everyday life. It can be a struggle. I admire your readiness to share what's been happening. I also admire everything you have been doing to keep your family strong despite the challenges.

Note my willingness to reveal information about myself and my feelings. I, too, grapple with challenges of raising children in our modern world. Many therapists choose to avoid sharing personal information. I find that self-disclosure can be incredibly helpful when it is carefully considered and purposeful. It helps parents to feel less alone in their struggles and more comfortable opening up. Sharing a part of myself helps parents to see me as a real person, and it energises the space between us. It also strengthens my relationships with parents and gives them hope.

There are times when parents thank me profusely for improvements in their child. The mother of a 14-year-old girl who had struggled with anxiety told me that: "She's not as anxious. She's really doing ok. She's becoming much more independent. We couldn't have done it without you." I thanked her, before reminding her that it was her daughter and herself, not me, who had really done the work. When all is said and done, lasting change comes from within families.

3 Encourage Regular Rituals of Connection

> The family that eats together stays together.
> Unknown

A few suggestions about supporting families. Avoid generic statements to parents about the importance of family. Encourage practices that contribute to family wellbeing. For example, regular family mealtimes. As I've said before, emphasise the fact that the parents know their children and their families best. I've found statements such as the following to be helpful:

> I understand that you feel deeply concerned about your child. You've explained that you feel overwhelmed and frustrated. Having regular family activities can help children – and parents – to cope with any difficult feelings they might be experiencing and to feel better because they help everyone to feel supported. You know this. Some parents tell me that having regular mealtimes or regular one-on-one time or reading together can be helpful. You know your family best. I want to talk about your current family activities, and explore some possible new family activities. I want to go over what you think would be most helpful for your family.

Regular family activities and gatherings can reduce stress because they reinforce the idea that the family is a reliable source of support. Clinical and developmental psychologist Barbara H. Fiese has studied family routines and rituals and how these practices impact child development and family health. Two decades ago, Fiese and her colleagues wrote that: "The emotional bonds created during these repetitive gatherings are played over and over again in memory, contributing to a sense that individuals belong to a group that can be a safe refuge" (Fiese et al. 2006, p. 69). In our time of rapid change and global uncertainty, consistent family touchpoints have never been more important.

When our children were very young, Michael and I had 10 to 20 minutes of one-on-one time with each of our children most days. We had two rules: our children got to choose what we did and no devices. I have tender memories of doing drawings, building towers, and playing card games together. When they each turned seven, we started having what we call one-on-one birthday mini-breaks. It is a precious family tradition in which Michael or I spend a weekend away with each of our three children in turn at around the time of their birthdays. We set off from our home in the Dandenong Ranges to places like Melbourne, Gippsland, and the Mornington Peninsula. Each of our trips is a great adventure, and they help Michael and me to connect more deeply with each child.

Murrundindi often speaks about the power of yarning circles to cement family ties. One of our conversations about yarning circles went like this:

"What would you say to parents who might be interested in having regular circles with their children?" I asked.

"It brings the family together in one circle," Murrundindi said. "Being in a circle, you can open up and speak from your heart."

"You've told me before that you have yarning circles with your family every week. Tell me more about that."

"I do this at my house every Friday," he replied. "We talk about any little problems we've got going on."

I nodded.

"We pass a yarning stick around. You hold it in your hands, and you stop and think. Holding the yarning stick gives you the right to speak. Yarning sticks have been passed around in my culture for thousands and thousands of years. By sitting in a circle, we're looking at one another. We've got nothing to hide. We're amongst family."

"Why do you think yarning circles are so helpful, especially when people are having difficulty coping?" I asked.

"It gives everyone a chance to speak about how they feel from their heart. It gives children the confidence to speak more openly. It opens you up. You can open up and express how you are feeling. It helps for healing to speak up. It's a powerful thing to do. You're opening up, and you're connecting with one another. By speaking and opening up amongst your family, they can get you through the difficult times in life. It's about helping one another on their journey in life, I reckon. And when you listen to each other, well, that's how you learn."

I nodded again.

"But the most important thing is, you've got to open up, and get it out and off your chest. Because it's no good bottling it all up inside. You get anger inside you. There's no place for anger in your body. So, you've got to get that out."

Return, one final time, to Mila, a 14-year-old client with a history of family conflict. I tried to help her parents to become aware of the impact of their behaviour on Mila and to see the value of spending regular uninterrupted time with Mila. I urged them to try having more family time with Mila, and we mapped out a possible schedule. I've never forgotten her Mum's comments a few months later:

"We watch a Netflix movie on Friday nights. We are watching the whole series of *The Babysitters Club* on Saturday nights. She likes roller skating with her Dad every Sunday. My husband is better at that. She looks forward to that. She actually likes having time with us."

Their new family rituals had helped them to rebuild their once-troubled and tension-filled bonds into more loving relationships.

4 Encourage Messages of Love

> i carry your heart with me (i carry it in my heart)
> E. E. Cummings, *Complete Poems, 1904–1962* (p. 766)
> (Cummings 1991; originally published in 1973)

> ...the parents' primary task beyond providing for the child's survival, is to emanate a simple message to the child in word, deed, and (most of all) energetic presence, that he or she is precisely the person they love, welcome, and want.
> Gabor Mate, *The Myth of Normal* (p. 127)
> (Mate 2022)

Many years ago, Harry Stack Sullivan, the influential American psychiatrist, taught us that mental health is deeply influenced by our interpersonal relationships, especially during childhood (Sullivan 1955). Our sense of self is not innate, but rather it is developed through our relations with others. When we feel secure and nurtured in our relationships, we can grow and learn. Children need positive affirmations from those they love.

In his seminal book, *The Developing Mind: How Relationships and the Brain Interact to Shape Who We Are*, Daniel J. Siegel brings together neuroscience, attachment theory, and developmental psychology and writes that "human connections shape neural connections, and each contributes to mind" (Siegel 2015; p. 3). He points out that certain parenting practices, including affirmations of love, can support healthy brain development and emotional health. As he and Tina Payne Bryson say in *The Whole-Brain Child*: "Research studies have consistently shown that when parents offer repeated, predictable experiences in which they see and sensitively respond to their children's emotions and needs, their children will thrive" (Siegel and Bryson 2011, p. 143).

We child therapists need to ask parents: "How do you express affection to your child?" "Do you give your child cuddles or high fives? "Do you say, 'I love you' or use words of endearment?" "Do you write cards or loving messages?" I encourage parents to convey their love for their children openly and often. I sometimes suggest letters or messages on sticky notes. Now and then, I share with parents that I write a birthday letter to each of my children each year in what I call their "birthday books." These letters detail the year that was. I recount their significant life events and experiences, and I end each letter with these words: "I am so lucky to be your Mum."

Each year, I teach a course on *Working with Groups* at the University of Melbourne. I talk about the fundamentals of group and family therapy. The highlight for students is observing a family therapy role-play session with three guest actors, Jock Macneish, Simone Kiefer, and Tommy Macneish, playing the roles of Dad, Mum, and son. As the session unfolds, the family members invariably display destructive communication practices, such as blaming ("It's all your fault"), labelling ("You're a failure"), and judging ("You never do anything right"). Towards the end of the session, I encourage each family member to describe a time when they felt connected as a family and why. I also ask them to take turns expressing something they appreciate or admire about the other family members. Afterwards, I invite the actors and the students to discuss what they noticed about the family's communication (both verbal and nonverbal), what messages they were sending to each other, and whether any specific moments stood out. All agree that there is a noticeable shift when the family members tell family stories of connection and give each other compliments, even begrudgingly. It softens their hearts. The act of giving and receiving compliments is energising. It has a powerful impact on family relationships.

Messages of love are important. Children need to know that they are lovable. After I encouraged the mother of a 12-year-old girl to clearly demonstrate her love for her daughter, she told me that, “We now send love messages by text. Lots of hugging and cuddles—my husband is too. It’s made a big difference.” Urie Bronfenbrenner put it beautifully when he said, “Every child needs at least one adult who is irrationally crazy about him or her.”

5 Encourage Parents to Take Care of Themselves

> When our children are suffering, we suffer. When our children aren’t hurting, parenting can be difficult enough. Sometimes it feels as if we are hanging by a thread.
> Myla Kabat-Zinn and Jon Kabat-Zinn, *Everyday Blessings: The Inner Work of Mindful Parenting* (p. 352)
> (Kabat-Zinn and Kabat-Zinn 2014)

> Self-compassion is essential for good parenting. By being compassionate to ourselves, we can better handle the frustrations and difficulties of parenting…
> Kristen Neff, *Self-Compassion: The Proven Power of Being Kind to Yourself* (p. 207)
> (Neff 2011)

One afternoon, I met with Aisha, aged 15, and her Mum, Mariam. Aisha was having frequent episodes that looked like epileptic seizures, but they did not seem to have a physical cause. After conducting many tests, her neurologist said that they might be due to stress. I asked Aisha to tell me about the episodes, and I asked her about their impact. She described tingling sensations, difficulty speaking, and shortness of breath, and it was clear that the episodes were affecting Aisha deeply. She feared being out of control and worried about the effect they were having on her friends who had witnessed them. She was also anxious about her grades due to missing a lot of school.

I guessed that Mariam was experiencing many feelings, including helplessness, anxiety, fear, and exhaustion from constantly being on alert.

When Aisha left the room to use the bathroom, I said, "It must be hard for you to see Aisha struggle like this." I then asked what she was doing to take care of herself, and she looked puzzled. The question had caught her off guard. She hadn't stopped to think about her own wellbeing in the midst of caring for Aisha. A wave of gratitude swept over her face. Her own struggles and efforts had been recognised. This mother needed to be validated. She also needed to be reminded of the importance of meeting her own needs and taking some time for herself. I asked her what usually helped her to recharge her batteries. After a pause, she said, "Gardening."

"I would like to make a suggestion," I said. "See if you can take time out each week to garden. Next time we meet, I want to talk about that."

Many parents lose sight of the fact that they need nurturing too. In today's world, parents often face significant pressures, including work-life balance struggles, information overload, and financial stress. They are constantly exposed to images of seemingly "perfect" families, and they can be overly critical of themselves and feel inadequate when their children are struggling: "Other parents seem to have it all together. I can't have a break. There's too much to do." Many parents, especially new ones, prioritise their children's needs above their own, and it can come as a surprise when they are reminded of the vital importance of nourishing themselves.

As I write this section, I think of my years working as a school psychologist with Annette Rome at St Margaret's Berwick Grammar. Annette is one of the most eminent principals in Australia. She is warm, friendly, and super smart. She always dresses in flowing fabrics and wears strange and wonderful jewellery collected from a lifetime of travelling. I vividly recall a meeting with Annette and a parent, Samira, in March 2022. At this time, parents were slowly being allowed back onsite at schools after COVID-19 restrictions. We sat in upholstered antique chairs in Annette's office wearing facemasks. Samira's young daughter was a handful, and her husband worked out of town. Money was very tight. Samira had a demanding job and was struggling with being a parent. After reviewing how we might support Samira's daughter, Annette ended the hour by asking Samira: "And who is looking after you?" Samira started crying. She had been trying so hard to do everything, and she was overwhelmed and anxious. She reached for the tissues. She knew that she needed to take care of herself. "I think of my aunt. I can talk to her on the phone. She looks after me."

I loved the way Annette highlighted that we need support as parents. Daniel J. Seigel often speaks about raising children in community. Being a parent isn't a solo pursuit. It is not meant to be done in isolation. Parents do better and children do better when parents are surrounded by other supportive adults. In her book, *Mothers and Others: The Evolutionary Origins of Mutual Understanding*, American sociobiologist Sarah Blaffer Hrdy writes that humans are primed by evolution to need a lot of support (Hrdy 2011). Parents and families need support in order to survive and thrive. I recommend that parents create their own support group if they don't have an extended and supportive family. It took our ancient ancestors a village, and it takes modern parents a village to raise children. We child therapists need to encourage parents to go out and find their village.

PART IV

The World

CHAPTER 10

Expanding the Therapeutic Lens to Include the Wider World

1 Expand Your Focus to Include Each Child's World

> In our modern isolated societies we have gained technological advances; however, we have lost the salubrious climate of belonging, of support from others in our community.
> Peter Levine, *An Autobiography of Trauma* (p. 104)
> (Levine 2024)

Many adults believe that a child's struggles are due to something happening within the child. In my early years of clinical practice, I soon learned that children with complex problems are often experiencing difficulties within their family or their school life or both. Family dynamics and the wider world have a substantial impact on the mental health and wellbeing of children. It is often the environment that is the source of their problems.

A study in my home state of Victoria found that around one in four young Victorians experience a significant degree of loneliness and that those who are lonely are at increased risk of poorer mental health (Lim et al. 2019). I think that most children in therapy are lonely. According to my Australian Pocket Oxford Dictionary, the word lonely means "without

M. Andrews Luke, *A Guide to Relationship-Oriented Child Therapy*, Palgrave Texts in Counselling and Psychotherapy,
https://doi.org/10.1007/978-3-031-99658-0_10

companions" and "sad because of this" (2019). We all experience loneliness sometimes. Children who experience loneliness feel separate from the people around them. Sometimes they feel left out and excluded. They often feel different and misunderstood. I remember one child saying to me, "I don't feel like I belong in this world."

There are many reasons why children experience loneliness. A change of school, the death of a loved one, not getting along with family and friends, and being bullied are examples of situations that can trigger loneliness in children. In our contemporary society, a lack of extended family connections, fewer interactions with neighbours, and less opportunities to take part in community events can all lead to a sense of isolation. I also believe that social media use can exacerbate feelings of loneliness for some young people. One teenager told me that, "Everyone else seems to be having so much fun" and "I never get as many likes."

We child therapists need to examine how children's feelings of despair fit within the context of their lives. We must not lose sight of the influence of the environment. To find out about the worlds of his adult patients, Irvin Yalom always asked his patients to give him a detailed account of a typical day (Yalom 2002). When I meet with children, I usually ask them to draw their day: "Draw what you did today." "Draw what you did yesterday." "Can you show me your day in a drawing?" I sometimes invite children to make a collage of their day using old magazines and catalogues. "Can you cut out pictures and stick them together to show me your day?" "Tell me a story about your day using pictures." A 15-year-old boy chose pictures of devices and said that he spent many hours alone each night watching pornography on his phone. I also find it instrumental to ask: "What do you want your day to look like?" A 12-year-old girl whose parents worked long hours chose pictures of families spending time together in nature.

As children draw and cut out pictures, I place great importance on asking them how their lives are populated. "Who do you eat with?" "Who do you play with?" "Who do you spend time with on weekends?" "Who are your friends?" Another useful technique is to invite children to use sticky notes to create a visual representation of the groups they belong to. The child is asked: "What family groups are you part of?" "What groups are you part of at school?" "What groups do you belong to outside of school?" "How close do you feel to the groups?" Rich information emerges through this exercise. "I just want to be closer to my friends," said one 13-year-old girl.

We child therapists work with children hour after hour. We give children a calm space in which to express their fears and to consider the possibilities. We help by listening deeply and by asking good questions. Sometimes we offer suggestions. As well as attending closely to each child's inner world, we must also attend to their outer world, which profoundly shapes their experiences. By attending to both, we gain a more complete picture of each child's needs. And by showing a deep interest in each child's family dynamics, their school life, their friends, and their community, we also do much to strengthen our bond.

2 Understand How Schools Work

> Since children spend most of their time in school, it seems logical to me that all the people who work with children outside of the school setting ought to take the time to find out what schools are like for children today. Our own school experiences, if not forgotten, may have been quite different.
> Violet Oaklander, *Windows to Our Children* (p. 311)
> (Oaklander 2007; originally published in 1978)

Many children who come to therapy do not enjoy school. Some of my clients are concerned about keeping up with their homework. Others feel stressed about tests and exams. A large number worry about how they are perceived by their peers. A fair few say that they are bored: "School is boring!" Research by psychological scientist and educational researcher Reinhard Pekrun has shown that boredom is one of the most frequently experienced emotions in school settings (Pekrun and Linnenbrink-Garcia 2014). A study of Year 11 students found that they were bored in class more than half of the time (Nett, Goetz and Hall 2010).

As I write this section, I think about a bright and highly bored 16-year-old client, Jack. He avoided doing his homework and was not interested in his subjects: "I don't particularly enjoy them." When I asked Jack to say more, he said:

"Everyone says that I'm not meeting my potential, and that I could do better. I want to do better, but I put off work for days and days. I feel really bad about myself. I just want to have something I enjoy. I want to feel satisfied with myself."

I asked Jack to choose a colour to represent how he felt about his schoolwork. He chose brown: "It's dull." Jack had little choice over his subjects, and he was not able to pursue his own interests, such as his deep and enthusiastic interest in philosophy. He struggled to make a personal connection with his schoolwork, and he was tuned out. The standardised approach to learning was not working for Jack. It is no wonder that Jack was disengaged. One size does not fit all.

Schools have changed rapidly during my career. In Australia, there is now a mandated curriculum, an increased focus on formal tests and numerical data, a greater reliance on screens, less free time for students, and there are more teacher shortages. A 2022 study of Australian teachers by researchers at Monash University notes that a concerning number of teachers are leaving the profession and that 20% plan to leave within five years (Longmuir, Cordoba et al. 2022).

Since schools play an integral role in the lives of our clients, I recommend that you find out as much as you can about what is happening in schools today. Read reports by government education departments and research institutions, such as the Australian Council for Educational Research (ACER). I attend the University of Melbourne Faculty of Education Dean's Lecture Series, which is a series of public talks about education in Australia and throughout the world. The talks cover many issues, including educational disparities and assessment in education, and they stretch from new research findings to new practices in teaching and learning. I watch them online if I can't attend in person. I am often struck by the wisdom and passion of the speakers. I choose to attend the Dean's Lecture Series not only to learn as much as possible about the difficulties and opportunities in schools right now but also to help me to connect more deeply with my clients.

I also recommend that you take the time to schedule an appointment with your clients' teachers if you can. I have known child therapists who haven't set foot in a school setting for years. In my view, making a point of meeting with my clients' teachers and having a classroom visit early on is always valuable. Since I prefer to be as transparent as possible, I discuss this possibility with my clients and their families from the outset. Children rarely object to classroom visits. More often than not they are pleased. If I decide that it is time for a classroom visit, we discuss the purpose and the best time for a visit, usually before school or after school hours. I usually meet with their teacher one-on-one. Occasionally, my clients meet me with their teacher. Invariably, these visits lead to a new way of seeing my clients. As Mary Pipher notes:

> It helps therapists to remember that our theories come from a stilted clinical perspective. When people come to see us, they are at their most intense. When I see my clients in the real world, I realize how distorted our office view can be. (Pipher 1996) (p. 29)

By visiting our clients' classrooms and meeting with their teachers, we send our clients the message that we want to know them and their world better, and we gain precious information about our clients.

3 Support Children to Connect with Others

> We want our clients connected to us, their families, and to other people.
> Mary Pipher, *Letters to a Young Therapist* (p. 47)
> (Pipher 2016; originally published in 2003)

We can help our clients to cope with their struggles by being a calm presence. But if we want our clients to experience meaningful change, we must support our clients to connect with the people around them. There are many ways to help our clients to have stronger relationships. For one, keep in mind that simply communicating our deep acceptance of our clients and who they are assists our clients to feel freer to express themselves and to be more authentic, both with us and in their other relationships. Validate their experiences. Treat them the way you would like to be treated. Trust in their capacity for growth. Respect their wisdom. At the end of the day, the positive client-therapist relationship itself is a catalyst for positive relationships outside of the therapy room. When we help our clients to feel fully seen, heard, understood, and valued, our clients feel less alone in their fears and more confident to join in with others.

Throughout the course of therapy, I also ask my clients how those around them might see things. I invite children to draw how they are with their friends and family and to draw the impact of their actions on others. If they have told me about a troubling interpersonal situation, I might say: "Draw what happened." "Tell me what you are doing in your drawing. Tell me what everyone else is doing." "How does everyone feel?" I sometimes invite children to close their eyes and to imagine their day: "Close your eyes and picture what you did today. Picture what you could see, hear, smell, and touch." "Tell me a bit about what you did." "What did it feel like for you? What did it feel like for the people around you?" I previously mentioned the empty chair technique developed by Fritz Perls. It can be most useful: "Imagine your Mum sitting in that empty chair. If your Mum was sitting there listening to you right now, what would she say?" Many of our clients have difficulties with relationships and struggle to be empathic. By asking these questions, we help our clients to consider different perspectives. Walking in the shoes of others is at the heart of relating well to others.

Sometimes our clients must be guided more directly. I often encourage my clients to role play new ways of relating to others and to experiment with putting these behaviours into practice. An example: a 13-year-old boy, Aaron, sought my assistance because the thought of attending school camp made him worried.

"I'm a little bit scared. And a little bit scared of being left out. Standing alone. Not talking to anyone. Being on the outside," Aaron said.

"We could think of your time at camp as an experiment. What would it be like to talk to some new people on camp, as an experiment?" I asked.

"I guess I could try talking to new people who I haven't talked to before," Aaron said.

"How confident are you about talking to new people, out of 10?" I asked.

"Six out of 10. It's hard to talk to other people," he responded.

For the rest of our session, we role-played what the conversations might look like. The next time Aaron met with me he informed me that he initially felt nervous about talking to new people, but that he found it enjoyable overall: "I came back from camp quite happy." A study by behavioural scientists Juliana Schroeder, Donald Lyons, and Nicholas Epley found that London train commuters who talked to strangers felt happier but may have felt concerned about starting a conversation. Our clients might avoid initiating social contact because they overestimate the potential pitfalls and underestimate the advantages. Good child therapists try to help children to reach out to others because connecting with others is ultimately a source of wellbeing. As the researchers note, "Human beings are inherently social such that connecting with others - even with complete strangers - reliably increases people's moods" (Schroeder et al. 2021, p. 1141).

4 Help Each Child to Help Others

> A man who becomes conscious of the responsibility he bears toward a human being who affectionately waits for him, or an unfinished work, will never be able to throw away his life. He knows the 'why' for his existence, and will be able to bear almost any 'how.'
> Viktor E. Frankl, *Man's Search for Meaning* (p. 107)
> (Frankl 2020; originally published in German in 1946)

Viktor Frankl's most famous book, *Man's Search for Meaning*, has always stuck with me (Frankl 2020; originally published in German in 1946). In it, he describes his time in concentration camps during World War II and his approach to therapy. He wrote it in nine consecutive days. It is the most compelling story of overcoming adversity I have ever read. Frankl explains that suffering is part of being human and that the prisoners who were able to focus on searching for meaning and purpose in life had a greater chance of survival. He writes about one case of would-be suicide whose love for his child gave him strength, even in the most horrific of circumstances. He writes about another case of would-be suicide whose dedication to finishing a series of books gave him a reason to persevere. By loving and serving others, we can find meaning, purpose, strength, and hope in the face of despair.

Positive psychologist Evelyn Rosset and her colleagues suggest that taking care of others allows us to better take care of ourselves (Rosset, El-Jor et al. 2024). They challenge the idea that one should take care of oneself in order to better take care of others and propose what they refer to as an other-oriented model of wellbeing or "taking care of oneself *through* taking care of others" (p. 2). Studies show that supporting others benefits us enormously. Research by social neuroscientist Tristen Inagaki demonstrates that the act of giving support is associated with lower inflammation throughout the body (Inagaki, Alvarez et al. 2023) and reduced stress-related neural activity (Inagaki, Haltom et al. 2016). Caring for others is good for our health. It helps us to feel better. The Dalai Lama said, "If you want others to be happy, practice compassion. If you want to be happy, practice compassion."

Of course, good child therapists help children to feel better about themselves by helping them to take care of themselves and, if it feels right, to care for others. Sometimes, helping our clients to focus on others is what is needed. So where can child therapists start? We can support children to think about how others feel and to recognise opportunities for kindness. We might ask our clients: "Who are you grateful for? Why?" "Is there someone in your life you'd like to thank? How could you thank them?" "What's something nice you could do for someone this week?" When I work with younger children, I find that sentence starters are helpful: "I am grateful for..." "I want to thank..." I sometimes invite children to draw a picture of kindness. I might ask: "Who can you be kind to today?" Being kind and generous towards others energises us.

While writing this, I am reminded of a 13-year-old girl, Anna, whose older sister died unexpectedly.

Anna said in a low voice, "I can feel the first anniversary getting close. It's hard for my family."

"Tell me more," I said.

"There's a lot of sadness. My parents' pain is different to my pain. I help my parents a bit. I've been helping around the house, making sure everything is neat and tidy and clean. I want to be there for my parents. This is how I like to approach things".

Oftentimes, the cure for sadness is service towards others. Doing good helps to lift our spirits. Children are at their best when they are helping others. They feel purposeful and more satisfied, and they see themselves more clearly. It was Mahatma Gandhi who once said: "The best way to find yourself is to lose yourself in the service of others."

5 Collaborate with Teachers

> A child becomes what he experiences. While parents possess the original key to their offspring's experience, teachers have a spare key. They, too, can open or close the minds and hearts of children.
> Haim Ginott, *Teacher and Child: A Book for Parents and Teachers* (p. 233) (Ginott 1975)

In Australia, children typically spend 6 to 6.5 hours in school each day. The school day usually begins between 8:30am and 9:00am and ends between 3:00pm and 3:30pm. Teachers, not therapists, have daily contact with children. They see children in different situations. Every day, teachers observe children learning, communicating, socialising, problem-solving, and exploring. They are a constant presence in our clients' lives.

Teachers know children, and they notice changes in children's mood and behaviour. Teachers are often the first to see signs of distress. They are also in the best position to be there for our clients, day in and day out.

I previously wrote about scheduling an appointment early on with your clients' teachers. It worries me that many child therapists do not collaborate with teachers. If we child therapists are to truly understand our clients and develop a deep appreciation of their needs and experiences, then it stands to reason that we must be willing to work in partnership with their teachers. Therapy is just one component of our clients' lives. Teachers can give us child therapists a better picture of our clients' difficulties and strengths, which can help us to better support our clients. Teachers can also help our clients to feel more positive about themselves.

When I meet with a teacher, I ask them to describe the child. I might say: "Tell me about the child." "What do they find most challenging at school?" "How do they relate to their peers?" "How do they relate to you?" "What are the child's strengths?" I frequently find myself asking for more specific details: "Tell me more." Meeting with teachers helps me to decide where to begin my work with the child.

In my conversations with teachers, I describe what I am doing with the child and my rationale. I introduce my ideas about helping each child to feel seen, heard, and accepted by others, and the importance of helping each child to have caring relationships so that they may flourish. I outline the steps I personally take to tune into each child, to walk in each child's shoes, and to listen deeply to each child. Although teachers are not therapists, they can still use and adapt these skills in their interactions with each child. I am yet to meet a teacher who is not open to discovering new ways of connecting with and helping children.

Even though the teachers I work with are keen to learn more about how to relate well to each child, some teachers tell me that they feel exasperated by their workload. Others say that they feel ill-equipped to support children's wellbeing and mental health in addition to their teaching and administrative duties. In the 2022 study of Australian teachers I described earlier, most of the teachers (86.1%) said that the amount of work they had to do was unmanageable (Longmuir, Cordoba et al. 2022). Many teachers in this study also noted that working with other professionals such as counsellors would help to reduce their workload.

While I am acutely aware that teacher stress is a serious problem that cannot be fixed easily, one benefit of child therapists collaborating with teachers is that it alleviates some of the pressure and helps teachers to feel supported. This in turn has far-reaching impacts on the ability of teachers to support students. In her book, *Contextual Wellbeing: Creating Positive Schools from the Inside Out*, Helen Street makes the following remarks: "when school staff experience a state of wellbeing, with manageable stress levels and social and emotional competency, they can more effectively support positive relationships and social emotional learning in their students" (Street 2018, p. 111). Supported teachers support students.

Collaborating with teachers can be a game-changer. Here are some statements by teachers about the benefits of collaboration between child therapists and teachers:

> "To collaborate with a mental health professional who specialises in helping children is extremely beneficial for a teacher" (Sue Eden, Early Learning Centre Director).
> "Collaborating with child therapists has provided essential support and insight into my own practice as a teacher. I also feel emotionally supported by the therapist as quite often I am needing some understanding and guidance to help with children's behaviours in the classroom. Working with child therapists is a chance to seek expert advice and work together on strategies to try in the classroom. It also helps me feel seen and heard. People forget how much time a child is with a teacher in class every week" (Tracey Sawyers, Early Learning Centre teacher).
> "Child therapists are a resource. They are great to bounce off ideas. They provide different strategies you may not have considered. They enable everyone to share observations and develop an understanding of the whole child. Everyone is on the same page, and everyone supports each other" (Karryn Exner, Prep teacher).
> "We develop a shared language around the child's current challenges and areas for growth. I am better able to support the student throughout the day. It is also a place to celebrate successes" (Sara Powell, Year 1 teacher).
> "Teachers can learn effective strategies from professionals. It helps me to ensure that all students have the opportunity to achieve success. I can make sure the learning experiences are inclusive and the students develop a sense of belonging" (Bridget Stein, Year 4 teacher).
> "It gives me a better understanding of young people, their vulnerabilities, and their ways of being" (Kate Bartholomeusz, Year 6 teacher).
> "The biggest advantage I have found working with a child's therapist is a better understanding of the child's needs. Through this, I get to tailor my teaching approach. Working with the therapist can also help teachers to recognise and address any difficulties and provide early intervention to assist with any concerns" (Michael Davies, Year 6 teacher).

> "Collaboration between classroom teachers and child therapists greatly benefits the child. Teachers, who spend significant time with their students, develop a deep understanding of their students' needs and behaviors. This insight helps therapists gain a more comprehensive understanding of the child, allowing them to provide more effective support. In addition, the teachers can learn from child therapists about implementing various strategies and how to provide the appropriate emotional support for the child" (Linzy Pattison, Year 6 teacher).

"Collaborate" comes from the Latin verb "collaborare." It combines the prefix "col-," which means "together" or "with," and "laborare," which means "to work." In simple terms, to collaborate with teachers means to work together with them to provide the best possible care for the child. The more we child therapists know about each child's world, the more we can enter their world and develop a deep connection with each child. Working with teachers improves the client-therapist relationship.

Conclusion

I love working as a child therapist, and I love working as a teacher and clinical supervisor of beginning child therapists. I started out writing this book for new child therapists, but I also hope it will be a valuable guide for more experienced therapists. There are far too few of us child therapists and far too few books on the work of child therapy and what actually happens in child therapy. I was keen to share examples from my own practice. I wanted to give therapists some practical ideas about how to connect with children and how to make therapy work. Our world needs more therapists who are willing to work with children, their families, and their teachers, and who approach their work with confidence in themselves and in the healing power of relationships. I wrote this book because I wanted to support therapists who support children.

I write to think, and each time I sat down to write, I made new discoveries and deepened my understanding of the therapeutic process. I learned a lot. Writing helped to refine and organise my ideas. It is my hope that reading my suggestions helped you to clarify your thoughts about how to help children cope.

As I conclude this book, my key message is that effective child therapy is about listening well to children so that they feel seen, heard, and supported, and so that they may grow, develop, and connect meaningfully with those around them. Children, like all of us, want to have close

M. Andrews Luke, *A Guide to Relationship-Oriented Child Therapy*, Palgrave Texts in Counselling and Psychotherapy, https://doi.org/10.1007/978-3-031-99658-0

connections. Everything we do as child therapists should be in pursuit of this goal.

I trained as an educational and developmental psychologist, and I see children's challenges and growth in the context of their broader lives. Children do not exist in a vacuum. Our work should aim to link each child's challenges with what is happening in their environment and to nurture their relationships outside the therapy room. We can do this by simply listening to children and the people who populate their lives with our full selves.

Listening provides the space for greater awareness and better relationships. Let's listen to children and give them hope.

References

Ainsworth, M. D. S., & Bell, S. M. (1970). Attachment, exploration, and separation: Illustrated by the behavior of one-year-olds in a strange situation. Child Development, 41(1), 49–67.

Ainsworth, M. D. S., Blehar, M. C., Waters, E., & Wall, S. N. (2015). Patterns of attachment: A psychological study of the strange situation. Psychology Press. (Original work published 1978)

Allen, P. (2000). Herbert & Harry. Puffin Books. (Original work published 1986)

Animal Medicines Australia. (2022). Pets in Australia: A national survey of pets and people.

Axline, V. M. (1950). Play therapy experiences as described by child participants. Journal of Consulting Psychology, 14(1), 53–63.

Axline, V. M. (1990). Dibs: In search of self: Personality development in play therapy. Penguin Books. (Original work published 1964)

Axline, V. M. (1990). Play therapy. Ballantine Books. (Original work published 1947)

Bland, N. (2008). The very cranky bear. Scholastic Press.

Blau, D. S. (2013). Clark E. Moustakas (1923–2012). American Psychologist, 68(5), 401.

Blyton, E. (2020). The magic faraway tree collection. Hodder Children's Books. (Original work published 1939–1946)

Bodie, G. D., St. Cyr, K., Pence, M., Rold, M., & Honeycutt, J. (2012). Listening Competence in Initial Interactions I: Distinguishing Between What

M. Andrews Luke, *A Guide to Relationship-Oriented Child Therapy*, Palgrave Texts in Counselling and Psychotherapy, https://doi.org/10.1007/978-3-031-99658-0

Listening Is and What Listeners Do. International Journal of Listening, 26(1), 1–28.
Bowlby, J. (2005). The making and breaking of affectional bonds. Routledge. (Original work published 1979)
Bratton, S. C., Ray, D., Rhine, T., & Jones, L. (2005). The efficacy of play therapy with children: A meta-analytic review of treatment outcomes. Professional Psychology: Research and Practice, 36(4), 376–390.
Britzman, D. P. (2016). Melanie Klein: Early analysis, play, and the question of freedom. Springer.
Bronfenbrenner, U. (1991). What do families do? Family Affairs, 4(1–2), 2.
Brontë, C. (2006). Jane Eyre. Penguin Books. (Original work published 1847)
Cohen, L. (1992). Anthem [Song]. On The future. Columbia Records.
Conroy, P. (1991). The prince of tides. Bantam Books.
Corey, G. (2020). Personal reflections on counseling. American Counseling Association.
Csikszentmihalyi, M. (2002). Flow: The classic work on how to achieve happiness. Random House. (Original work published 1990)
Csikszentmihalyi, Mihaly. *Flow*. London: Random House, 2002; originally published in 1992.
Cummings, E. E. (1991). Complete poems, 1904–1962 (G. J. Firmage, Ed.). Liveright Publishing Corporation. (Original work published 1973)
DeLoache, J. S., Pickard, M. B., & LoBue, V. (2011). How very young children think about animals. In P. McCardle, S. McCune, J. A. Griffin, & V. Maholmes (Eds.), How animals affect us: Examining the influences of human–animal interaction on child development and human health (pp. 85–99). American Psychological Association.
Dickinson, E. (1960). The complete poems of Emily Dickinson (T. H. Johnson, Ed.). Little, Brown and Company.
Dodd, H. F., & Lester, K. J. (2021). Adventurous play as a mechanism for reducing risk for childhood anxiety: A conceptual model. Clinical Child and Family Psychology Review, 24(1), 164–181.
Drake, J. E., & Winner, E. (2013). How children use drawing to regulate their emotions. Cognition and Emotion, 27(3), 512–520.
Duncan, B. L., Miller, S. D., Sparks, J. A., Claud, D. A., Reynolds, L. R., Brown, J., & Johnson, L. D. (2003). The Session Rating Scale: Preliminary psychometric properties of a "working" alliance measure. Journal of Brief Therapy, 3(1), 3–12.
Dweck, C. S. (2012). Mindset: The new psychology of success (Updated ed.). Random House. (Original work published 2006)
Einstein, A. (1929, October 26). What life means to Einstein: An interview by George Sylvester Viereck [Interview]. The Saturday Evening Post.
Eliot, G. (1857/n.d.). Scenes of clerical life. The Walter Scott Publishing Co.

Eliot, T. S. (2019). Four quartets. Faber & Faber. (Original work published 1943)
Erikson, E. H. (1987). Childhood and society. Paladin Grafton Books. (Original work published 1950)
Fiese, B. H., Foley, K. P., & Spagnola, M. (2006). Routine and ritual elements in family mealtimes: Contexts for child wellbeing and family identity. New Directions for Child and Adolescent Development, 2006(111), 67–90.
Fox, M. (2008). Ten little fingers and ten little toes (H. Oxenbury, Illus.). Penguin Books.
Fox, M. (2008). Possum magic (J. Vivas, Illus.). Scholastic Books. (Original work published 1983)
Frank, A. (2019). The diary of a young girl. Penguin Classics. (Original work published 1947)
Frankl, V. E. (2020). Man's search for meaning. Rider. (Original work published 1946)
Fredrickson, B. L. (2013). Love 2.0: Creating happiness and health in moments of connection. Penguin Group.
Frydenberg, E. (2018). Adolescent coping: Promoting resilience and well-being. Routledge.
Frydenberg, E. (2022). Coping in good times and bad: Developing fortitude. Melbourne University Press.
Frydenberg, E., & Deans, J. (2011). The early years coping cards [Card deck]. Australian Council for Educational Research.
Frydenberg, E., & Lewis, R. (2011). Adolescent Coping Scale-2 [Measurement instrument]. Australian Council for Educational Research.
Geldard, K., Geldard, D., & Foo, R. Y. (2018). Counselling children: An introduction. SAGE Publications. (Original work published 1997)
Gibson, E. C. (2023). Your family revealed: A guide to decoding the patterns, stories, and belief systems in your family. Sounds True.
Ginott, H. G. (1975). Teacher and child: A book for parents and teachers. Avon Books.
Goding, G. (1992). The history and principles of family therapy. Victorian Association of Family Therapy.
Goleman, D. (2006). Social intelligence: The new science of human relationships. Hutchinson.
Grimm, J., & Grimm, W. (2012). Little Red Riding Hood (B. Watts, Illus.). NorthSouth Books. (Original work published 1812)
Haidt, J. (2024). The anxious generation: How the great rewiring of childhood is causing an epidemic of mental illness. Penguin Press.
Havighurst, S. S., & Harley, A. (2007). Feeling faces [Poster]. In S. S. Havighurst & A. Harley (Eds.), Tuning in to kids: Emotionally intelligent parenting program manual. University of Melbourne.

Hesse, H. (2020). Siddhartha. Macmillan Collector's Library. (Original work published 1922)
Hill, E. M., An, M., Kivlighan, D. M., Jr., & Gelso, C. J. (2024). A tripartite model of the psychotherapy relationship: Interrelations among its components and their unfolding across sessions. Psychotherapy, 61(2), 151–160.
Homer. (1966). The Odyssey (E. V. Rieu, Trans.). Penguin Classics. (Original work published ca. 8th or 7th century BCE)
Horney, K. (1991). Neurosis and human growth: The struggle toward self-realization. W. W. Norton & Company. (Original work published 1950)
Hosokawa, R., Tomozawa, R., & Katsura, T. (2023). Associations between family routines, family relationships, and children's behavior. Journal of Child and Family Studies, 32(11), 3988–3998.
Hrdy, S. B. (2011). Mothers and others: The evolutionary origins of mutual understanding. Harvard University Press.
Inagaki, T. K., Alvarez, G. M., Orehek, E., Ferrer, R. A., Manuck, S. B., Abaya, N. M., & Muscatell, K. A. (2023). Support-giving is associated with lower systemic inflammation. Annals of Behavioral Medicine, 57, 499–507.
Inagaki, T. K., Byrne Haltom, K. E., Suzuki, S., Jevtic, I., Hornstein, E., Bower, J. E., & Eisenberger, N. I. (2016). The neurobiology of giving versus receiving support: The role of stress-related and social reward-related neural activity. Psychosomatic Medicine, 78(4), 443–453.
Innovative Resources. (2022). The bears [Card deck].
Innovative Resources. (2023). Strengths cards [Card deck].
Ironside, V. (2004). The huge bag of worries (F. Willems, Illus.). Hodder Children's Books.
James, W. (1890). The principles of psychology. Henry Holt and Company.
Jo, H., Song, C., Ikei, H., Enomoto, S., Kobayashi, H., & Miyazaki, Y. (2019). Physiological and psychological effects of forest and urban sounds using high-resolution sound sources. International Journal of Environmental Research and Public Health, 16(15), 2649.
Jung, C. G. (1933). Modern man in search of a soul. Kegan Paul, Trench, Trubner & Co.
Kabat-Zinn, J. (1994). Wherever you go, there you are: Mindfulness meditation in everyday life. Hyperion.
Kabat-Zinn, M., & Kabat-Zinn, J. (2014). Everyday blessings: The inner work of mindful parenting. Hachette Books.
Karen, R. "Becoming Attached." The Atlantic Monthly (1990, February): 1–18.
Karst, P. (2000). The invisible string (J. Lew-Vriethoff, Illus.). DeVorss & Company.
Kaufman, S. B. (2020). Transcend: The new science of self-actualization. TarcherPerigee.
Kornfield, J. (1994). Buddha's little instruction book. Bantam Books.

Lee, H. (1974). To kill a mockingbird. Pan Books. (Original work published 1960)

Lee, S. Y. (2013). "Flow" in art therapy: Empowering immigrant children with adjustment difficulties. Art Therapy: Journal of the American Art Therapy Association, 30(2), 56–63.

Levine, P. A. (2024). An autobiography of trauma: A healing journey. Park Street Press.

Lim, M. H., Eres, R., & Peck, C. (2019). The Young Australian Loneliness Survey: Understanding loneliness in adolescence and young adulthood. Victorian Health Promotion Foundation (VicHealth).

Lin, Y.-W., & Bratton, S. C. (2015). A meta-analytic review of child-centered play therapy approaches. Journal of Counseling & Development, 93(1), 45–58.

Longmuir, F., Gallo Cordoba, B., Phillips, M., Allen, K.-A., & Moharami, M. (2022). Australian teachers' perceptions of their work in 2022. Monash University.

Maslow, A. H. (1970). Motivation and personality (2nd ed.). Harper & Row.

Maslow, A. H. (1999). Toward a psychology of being (3rd ed.). John Wiley & Sons. (Original work published 1962)

Maté, G. (2022). The myth of normal: Trauma, illness and healing in a toxic culture. Random House.

Miller, S. D., & Duncan, B. L. (2000). The Outcome Rating Scale [Measurement instrument]. International Center for Clinical Excellence.

Miller, S. D., Duncan, B. L., & Johnson, L. (2000). The Session Rating Scale [Measurement instrument]. International Center for Clinical Excellence.

Minuchin, S. Families and Family Therapy. London: Tavistock Publications, 1974.

Minuchin, S., Reiter, M. D., & Borda, C. (2021). The craft of family therapy: Challenging certainties (2nd ed.). Routledge.

Moustakas, C. E. (1953). Children in play therapy. McGraw-Hill.

Neff, K. (2011). Self-compassion: The proven power of being kind to yourself. HarperCollins.

Nett, U. E., Goetz, T., & Hall, N. C. (2011). Coping with boredom in school: An experience sampling perspective. Contemporary Educational Psychology, 36(1), 49–59.

Nhat Hạnh, T. (1999). The heart of the Buddha's teaching: Transforming suffering into peace, joy, and liberation. Rider.

Norcross, J. C., & Alexander, E. F. (2019). A primer on psychotherapy integration. In J. C. Norcross & M. R. Goldfried (Eds.), Handbook of psychotherapy integration (3rd ed., pp. 3–23). Oxford University Press.

Norcross, J. C., & Lambert, M. J. (2018). Psychotherapy relationships that work III. Psychotherapy, 55, 303–315.

Oaklander, V. (2007). Windows to our children: A Gestalt therapy approach to children and adolescents. Gestalt Journal Press. (Original work published 1978)

Oxford University Press. (2019). Oxford dictionary (8th ed.) (M. Gwynn & A. Laugesen, Eds.).

Pearlman, L. A., & Mac Ian, P. S. (1995). Vicarious traumatisation: An empirical study of the effects of trauma work on trauma therapists. Professional Psychology: Research and Practice, 26, 558–565.

Pekrun, R., & Linnenbrink-Garcia, L. (Eds.). (2014). International handbook of emotions in education. Routledge.

Pipher, M. (1996). The shelter of each other. G. P. Putnam.

Pipher, M. (2016). Letters to a young therapist. Basic Books. (Original work published 2003)

Plastow, M. (2011). Hermine Hug-Hellmuth, the first child psychoanalyst: Legacy and dilemmas. Australasian Psychiatry, 19(3), 206–210.

Plath, S. (1965). Ariel. Faber and Faber.

Rideout, V., Peebles, A., Mann, S., & Robb, M. B. (2022). Common Sense census: Media use by tweens and teens. Common Sense.

Rilke, R. M. (2001). Letters to a young poet (R. Soulard Jr., Ed.). Burning Man Books. (Original work published 1929)

Rogatko, T. P. (2009). The influence of flow on positive affect in college students. Journal of Happiness Studies, 10(2), 133–148.

Rogers, C. R. (1942). Counseling and psychotherapy. The Riverside Press.

Rogers, C. R. (1961). On becoming a person: A therapist's view of psychotherapy. Houghton Mifflin Company.

Rosset, E., El-Jor, C., Kotsou, I., & Shankland, R. (2024). Getting outside of ourselves: Towards an other-oriented model of psychological health. International Journal of Wellbeing, 14(2), 1–19.

Ryan, R. M., & Deci, E. L. (2017). Self-determination theory: Basic psychological needs in motivation, development, and wellness. Guilford Press.

Satir, V. (1983). Conjoint family therapy. Science and Behavior Books. (Original work published 1964)

Schroeder, J., Lyons, D., & Epley, N. (2021). Hello, stranger? Pleasant conversations are preceded by concerns about starting one. Journal of Experimental Psychology: General, 151(5), 1141–1153.

Sendak, M. (2000). Where the wild things are. Random House. (Original work published 1963)

Shakespeare, W. (1895). The merchant of Venice (W. J. Rolfe, Ed.). Harper & Brothers. (Original work published 1600)

Shakespeare, W. Hamlet. London: Penguin, 2015; originally published in 1599.

Siegel, D. J. (2015). The developing mind: How relationships and the brain interact to shape who we are (2nd ed.). The Guilford Press.

Siegel, D. J., & Bryson, T. P. (2011). The whole-brain child: Twelve revolutionary strategies to nurture your child's developing mind. Random House.
Silverstein, S. (1992). The giving tree. HarperCollins. (Original work published 1964)
Skovholt, T. M., & Jennings, L. (2016). The cognitive, emotional, and relational characteristics of master therapists. In T. M. Skovholt & L. Jennings (Eds.), Master therapists: Exploring expertise in therapy and counseling (10th anniversary ed., pp. 31–52).
Skovholt, T. M., & Trotter-Mathison, M. (2025). The resilient practitioner: Burnout and compassion fatigue prevention and self-care strategies for the helping professions (4th ed.). Routledge.
Soneson, E., Puntis, S., Chapman, N., Mansfield, K. L., Jones, P. B., & Fazel, M. (2023). Happier during lockdown: A descriptive analysis of self-reported wellbeing in 17,000 UK school students during COVID-19 lockdown. European Child & Adolescent Psychiatry, 32(7), 1131–1146.
St Luke's Innovative Resources. (2001). Reflexions [Card deck].
Street, H. (2018). Contextual wellbeing: Creating positive schools from the inside out. Wise Solutions Books.
Sullivan, H. S. (1955). The interpersonal theory of psychiatry. Tavistock Publications.
Tolstoy, L. (1992). Anna Karenina. Barnes & Noble. (Original work published 1878)
Treleaven, D. A. (2018). Trauma-sensitive mindfulness: Practices for safe and transformative healing. W. W. Norton & Company.
van der Kolk, B. (2015). The body keeps the score: Brain, mind, and body in the healing of trauma. Penguin Books. (Original work published 2014)
Viorst, J. (1986). Alexander and the terrible, horrible, no good, very bad day (R. Cruz, Illus.). HarperCollins. (Original work published 1972)
von Bertalanffy, L. (1950). The theory of open systems in physics and biology. Science, 111(2872), 23–29.
Waldinger, R., & Schulz, M. (2023). The good life: Lessons from the world's longest study on happiness. Rider.
Waters, L. (2017). The strengths switch. Ebury Press.
Weinstein, N., Itzchakov, G., & Legate, N. (2021). The motivational value of listening during intimate and difficult conversations. Social and Personality Psychology Compass, 16(2), Article e12639.
Winnicott, D. W. (2021). The child, the family and the outside world. Penguin Classics. (Original work published 1957)
Wiener, N. (1948). Cybernetics: Or control and communication in the animal and the machine. Technology Press.
Winnicott, D. W. (2021). The child, the family, and the outside world. Penguin Classics. (Original work published 1957).

Woolf, V. (2022). Between the acts. Alma Classics. (Original work published 1941)
Yalom, I. D. (2002). The gift of therapy: Reflections on being a therapist (2nd ed.). Piatkus.
Yolen, J. (1987). Owl moon (J. Schoenherr, Illus.). Philomel Books.
Zaki, J. (2019). The war for kindness: Building empathy in a fractured world. Crown.

Index

M. Andrews Luke, *A Guide to Relationship-Oriented Child Therapy*, Palgrave Texts in Counselling and Psychotherapy,
https://doi.org/10.1007/978-3-031-99658-0

FSC
www.fsc.org
MIX
Papier | Fördert gute Waldnutzung
FSC® C083411

Kolibri 360 GmbH
Ferdinand-Jühlke-Straße 7
99095 Erfurt, Deutschland
produktsicherheit@kolibri360.de